INSIDE THE OUTSIDE

An Anthology of Avant-Garde American Poets

Cover Photos (l to r) *front*: Harry Smith, Lynne Savitt, Hugh Fox, A.D. Winans, John Keene, Kirby Congdon, Lyn Lifshin, Eric Greinke. *back*: Richard Kostelanetz, Doug Holder, Stanley Nelson, Mark Sonnenfeld, Richard Morris.

INSIDE THE OUTSIDE

An Anthology of Avant-Garde American Poets

Edited by
Roseanne Ritzema

Contributing Editors
Hugh Fox, Eric Greinke & Harry Smith

PRESA :S: PRESS

PRESA :S: PRESS
PO Box 792   Rockford, MI 49341
presapress@aol.com
www.presapress.com

Acknowledgments & Permissions

Some of these poems have been published previously in the following books & magazines & are reprinted by permission of the authors or the original publishers. **Stanley Nelson**: *Synesthetics/Edges of Sound* (Birch Brook Press, 2004). **Hugh Fox**: *Atom Mind*; *Aura Literary/Arts Review*; Cherry Valley Editions; Fat Frog Press; *Long Shot*; *Lynx Eye*; *The Plowman*; *The Sacred Cave & Other Poems* (Omega Cat Press, Cupertino, CA, 1992); Scars Publications; *Tears in the Fence*; Three-Legged Dog Press;; *Voices*; *Wobbley Zombies* (Goose River Press, 2004); Ye Olde Font Shoppe. **Kirby Congdon**: *Black Sun* (Pilot Press Books); *Boss*; *Cayo*; *The Christian Science Monitor*; *City*; *The Color of Gold*; *The Colorado Quarterly*; *Congress*; *Dream-Work* & *Novels* (Cycle Press); *The Dexter Review*; *Dimas*; *The Fiddlehead*; *The Heritage House Museum*; *Iron Ark* (Interim Books); *Kosmos*; *The Living Underground*; *Mouth of the Dragon*; *New*; *New to North America*; *The New York Times*; *One*; *Poetry Now*; *Presa*; *Quick Fiction*; *Selected Poems & Prose Poems* (Presa Press); & *Wordplay*. **Richard Kostelanetz**: *One-Word Poems*; *Wordworks* (Boa Editions, Limited). **Lyn Lifshin**: *40 Days Apple Nights*; *Black Apples* (The Crossing Press, NY, 1971); *Colors in Cooper Black* (Morgan Press, 1981); *Crazy Arms*, (Ommation Press, Chicago, 1977); *Ghost Dance*; *Hey Lady Supplement #15* (Morgan Press, 1971); *Moving by Touch* (Cotyledon Press, 1972); *North Poems* (Morgan Press, 1976); *Paper Apples*; *Why is the House Dissolving* (Open Skull Press, 1968); *Women Early Plymouth* (Morgan Press, 1977); *Wormwood Review*. **Harry Smith**: State of the Culture Press, 1979. **Eric Greinke**: *Abbey*; *Alcaeus Review*; *Bellevue Press Postcard Series*; *The Broken Lock* (Pilot Press Books, 1976); *The Cedar Rock Journal*; *The Detroit Free Press*; *The Goodly Co.*; *Ibbetson Street*; *The Iconoclast*; *Iron Rose* (Pilot Press Books, 1973); *The Last Ballet* (Pilot Press Books, 1972); *Mantras* (Floating Hair Press, 1973); *Napalm Health Spa Report 2005*; *Presa*; *Selected Poems 1972-2005* (Presa Press, 2005); *The Vagaries of Experience* (Sidewinder Press, 1982); *Windows In The Stone*. **John Keene**: *Aufgabe*; *Hambone*; *Indiana Review*; *New American Writing*; *Poems & Poets*; *Seismosis* (New York Center for Book Arts, 2004). **Lynne Savitt**: *13th Moon*; *The Burial Of Longing Beneath The Blue Neon Moon* (Ye Olde Fonte Shop, 1998); *Caprice*; *The Deployment Of Love In Pineapple Twilight* (Presa Press, 2005); *Dreams As Erect As Nipples On Ice* (Ghost Dance); *Eros Unbound* (Blue Horse Publications, 1980); *Greatest Hits 1979-2003* (Pudding House, 2004); *Home Planet News*; *Lust In 28 Flavors* (Second Coming Press, 1979); *New York Quarterly*; *No*

Apologies (Cardinal Press, 1981*); Plump Passions* (Ancient Mariners Press)*; Second Coming; Sleeping Retrospect Of Desire* (Konocti Books, 1993)*;Thundersandwich; The Transport Of Grandma's Yearning Vibrator (*Myskin Press). **A. D. Winans**: *13 Jazz Poems* (X-Ray Books); *Broadside* (Sore Dove Press, 2005); Centennial Press; *Dreams That Won't Let Me Alone (*Bottle of Smoke Press); *Main Street Rag; The Other Side of the Postcard* (City Lights Foundation); *The Pedestal Magazine; Poesy Magazine; Presa*; Pudding House Press; *Sleeping With Demons* (Mystery Island Publications); *This Land Is Not My Land* (24ᵗʰ Street Irregular Press). **Doug Holder:** *96inc..Magazine; "Dreams at the Au Bon Pain"* (Ibbetson, 2001)*; Facets Magazine; Hidden Oak; Lummox Journal; Poesy Magazine; Roswell Literary Review; Spare Change News; Wrestling With My Father(*Yellow Pepper Press, 2005). **Mark Sonnenfeld:** *3 + 3 + 3; A Green Shirted. mutiny. The Nose; A Red Shirted No Friends; Broadside, in by a janeway candlebox; Chapbook 6; da- de- vapor & spazz & on a snare perplexity; "Dash- - - "; East Windsor Studio; FILEx;in2;INDEPENDENT SMALL PUB.; 'November'; SURFACE; U g h; Writing sampler, Light in the Fall; Writing sampler, Sitting.* **Richard Morris:** *Ghost Dance.*

Desire by Eric Greinke is reprinted by permission of *The New York Quarterly.*

Introduction

Every 50 years or so, an anthology is produced which marks an epoch. *The New American Poetry* (ed. Donald Allen) appeared in 1960. The poets gathered in this volume represent the major schools of the American literary avant-garde as it has developed over the past 50 years. In virtually all areas of literary development, the truly progressive & ground-breaking work has been relegated to the small, independent publishers. Innovative writing breaks established rules, & charts out new territories. The large, commercial publishers, owned & operated by huge communications conglomerates, have published only what is deemed a safe investment, predictably appealing to the average reader. If a poetry reader seeks the avant-garde, he will have difficulty finding it on bookstore shelves, which are filled with the old boys of the upper class New England literary mafia, imitators of their parents' generation of post-war poets. The establishment turns a cold shoulder toward the children of Whitman, Dickinson & Poe, but the joke is on them.

Avant-garde poets may have a tendency to think of their own particular school of thought & practice to be *the* avant-garde, but the best of them appreciate their fellow outsiders, recognizing that they have in common a love of the art of poetry for itself, instead of as a means to fame or career.

Despite the diversity of the works presented here, the widely divergent methods used to create them & the philosophical & aesthetic differences between their creators, these poets have 3 fundamental things in common.

1). They all seek to break through barriers. Sometimes the barriers they confront may be relatively "accessible" to the reader. For example, Lifshin, Savitt & Holder seek to explore & experience psychological & emotional mysteries. The poets of social conscience (Morris, Congdon, Smith & Winans) also use normal colloquial speech patterns to confront social barriers.

Sometimes accessibility is more relative to the reader's mental flexibility than it is to the poem itself. Sometimes the works are profound in their reductionistic simplicity, as in Kostelanetz. Sometimes the works defy traditional rules of syntax or linear logic, as in the works of Keene, Nelson & Sonnenfeld.

Poets like Greinke & Fox use free association, stream-of-consciousness & imagery to represent alternative mental states such as revery, dream states or transcendental states.

2). All of these poets have been active in the small press movement, most as editors of literary magazines or as independent publishers. They are the founders & early members of COSMEP (Committee of Small Magazines Editors & Publishers) formed in 1968. They are the defenders of freedom of the press. They are the innovators who defied conventions & published the pure art, untinged by commercialism.

3). They tend to be influenced by sister-arts, such as painting, music & drama.

If a reader wants to see the new literature as it appears, he must subscribe to the independent literary magazines, the international network known variously as the small press, alternative press or independent presses. Over 4,000 of them can be found in the International Directory of Little Magazines & Small Presses (Dustbooks, PO Box 100, Paradise, CA 95967) published for over 40 years now by Len Fulton's Dustbooks. For his trouble, the reader will see what the vital grassroots poets of today are doing, & maybe experience new ways of thinking, feeling, & seeing within an expanded definition of poetry.

This volume brings together 13 major poets of the American small press scene, each representing an important branch of the avant-garde as it has developed over the past 50 years. Each of the poets is presented in a large section. In most cases, the poems were selected by the poets themselves.

They range in age from 41 to 81. Their poetics range from visual/conceptual poetry to surrealism, from personal/observation poetry to cut-up & collage poetry. Powerful, touching, innovative & humorous, this book illuminates the underground poetry scene to take the reader inside the outside of contemporary American poetry.

I wish to thank my contributing editors, Hugh Fox, Eric Greinke & Harry Smith, for their invaluable help in the initial selection of the poets for this anthology. There are other poets whose works could have been included here, but I am satisfied that the major schools have been represented while each poet's work has been given enough space to give the reader a basic experience of it.

Roseanne Ritzema
11/28/05

Contents

9

Richard Kostelanetz

Lyn Lifshin

Lynne Savitt

A. D. Winans

13

14

Richard Morris

Contributor's Notes................................297

for Richard Morris (1939 - 2003)
He served.

Stanley
Nelson

(1933 -   )

*Explores spatial placement of words on a page,
often breaking words themselves into discrete
sound-parts, evoking & creating perceptual
patterns that lead to fresh insights & meanings.*

The objective

flute

        flutters on its own breathing
        while the obedient

lute

        contributes its own
        fingers, all

embracing

        testing of deft and breath
        and the taste

(luminal)   of notes filched
        from ancient pottery

multichrom

        atic, the distanc
        ing echo of approach

such ef

        fortless breaching
        with breath and fingers

barricades

        mysteriously transparent, pil
        lared facades, the lute's

obedience

        sound, sound of approach (so
        very distant) as silt on castle

ledges

        or spurs on draw
        bridges, flutter

of phrases
            fetched from tapestry
            depicting sacred herds of

ibex
            or pancl of pliant noble
            women clutching golden

marmosets
            to archful cleavage, twinkle
            of touch and breath, inter

twine
            of dream and reverie calling
            the objective flute and obedient

lute to tunings ever

accessive to the sound, sound of approach, silt

ing

waves that purl on a shoreline

absent of creatures , advancing in luminous folds

to the base of the thug-headed heavy-lidded

idol whose orblike nostrils ache for human touch and
human

breath.

So Scriabin

broods on his mount
ain pon

        dering
        black con

        figurations—it is the

        black, the cracks
        between the black
        keys as he

ponders

        the bleak black pro
trusions in a sea of white

Scriab

        in, his

        mind

like a chessboard
set absently on a
pianotop, Scria

        bin's

pianotop
the Chopinesque black
candles—

        Maestro: tips

        of your vel
        vet sleeves touch

a sea of white

        filched
        fingers
        pilfer

bleak
        est
            black
                    est
           flame
                    fric
                          tion

of cabbalistic leaves
in a bog pin
        wheel
        (select
        an image)

spin
    ing
        spi
           raling

chasms convulse in multi
hues
        to elect elec
                trify
                    your senses

        nos
        trils
        yours, Scri
abin
        filled with the scent

of the rosy god

dess--in her ar
ousal she spills
all the seed of the world

in a single

Night.

The candles burn
down in their black
ness (will the Footman
come to replace them?)
and antipodal

Winds

claim their fire. Maestro, O Maestro:

Chaos

is your
Mother (though you have known

the clear sweet lakes of craters)

Fearsome

the Night-

Goddess, Pro

genetrix of chthonic
marionettes. Now

Breathe, Maestro

with the Nostrils
of the Cosmos

your fra

grant con
cantenation

rising to inflame

the Nostrils of the Cosmos

in

                    hail

        ing mul

                 titudenous

            stars   ex

   hal   ing

        um   bil

            ical

                              Worlds

Fables

"It is not fitting to feed a nightingale fables."
                        -Russian proverb

                fable(s)

            fit, are

        fit

        ed   to   nightynight

        in

                    gales: who (perhaps
                 John Keats) has spied them
                 Feeding on fables, feed

             ing
                    slight un

                    flighty fledglings
              hid in the thicket of

                        fa
                    bles bles re
                    cuperate among
                    the nightingales;

                    impoverished, dulled
                    the fables must not
                    dishonor

                                the nightynightin
                            gales: they must heal
                                    (in the thicket)

                    among the flip
                    floppity wings

                    in the deeper
                    foliage

                            where proverbs become
                    fairytales

               they must heal, the fables
               in the fluster of shielding

   wings, luster

                            25

less, stripped

of all reverb

eration

                                            soothing their wounds
                             among the birds, the
               birds

          of fable, fabl
          ed birds; they must,
          the fables, re

     cover their
luminosity, re
gain

                                        luster of wild
                               mushrooms on the
                            tundra, lust
          er of gem
and mineral

          until they are healed, the fables
robust and glowing - and they can fly!
                                    among
the nightingales

          hovering on the ledges of skyscrapers

          crest of a bridge, wood
          en platform of the el

       perching, the fables, on water
            tower and the metal domes
            of industrial waste plants

McDonalds, Mark's Diner, Columbus Circle
doppel

    gonging on the skaters in Central Park, gay
lovers on the Promenade

absorbent in the Cemetery of Colonial Graves

    gliding overnight to the fields of sparseness
    the waste places

    where the root, bitter and boot-
    trodden

      sprouts up and out
      to the light of the fables -

      wheeling them to remote
      caves of disintegration, re

incarnation
    transfiguration
    and now they are fit   *fit!*

      to be fed to
              nightingales.

Ah Browning

your frail cup
of three leaves of

ferring such
slight

ness to the cold
sun, must

have known
a season of

ascension   when your Sun
                        treader

emerged   from his siege of Isold
          ean Darkness

casting his largesse
abundant
          ly from Sky to Earth

Browning
          your flower
                    your dear
          win
                    ter flower

          grows alone among
          the reeds, sole

Survivor—
          and sun too

is frail,
          unspaced at its source as it seeks its own

Differentiation. Flower, sun, marshreed,
Earth—
          all that is—

                    awaits his

        Coming, Sun
                    treader

                    who knows the poetry

        of the Cosmos
        and will sing
        the slant

                    ing light

        out of its dark
        chamber, tilt

                    ing the song

        stations
                    toward the lit

        Spaces. emerge em
        erge
                out of con
                        can
                            te
                                national
        cy
            clonics
                        song-healing
        fragments
                        of the sun
                        singing beyond

                        the limitations
                        of the frag

                    29

ments
       of the lab
             yrinth
                  act
                      ualizing
attributes, manife

stations
        rescuing
            verycore

of the sun
        from uni
            versal labyrinths

sinuous your Song-
Spirals
        like white serpents
        in rapid flight

Swirling
        out of Blakean
            prophetics

Banners of
        Sunsound from
        your [throat-tongue] axis

Emanating
Sunriffs
        out of whirling
tet
    tra
        gram
            atons

wheeling
          with cheetah-breasted, falcon-
headed
          creatures of the sun

Awaken, Sun
               treader, crave

 and sparkle

Dawn
          before the sun

Elixir
               within the fire

Unfold
          the secret flower

your flower

Browning, your win

ter

     flower, valiant

     flower, golden

     flower

                    with its frail

                    cup of three leaves.

Note: in Browning's poem Pauline, Sun-treader represents the poet Shelley.

Yeats' gong

discs
>> Its sharpness into the hearts
>> of unyielding men

>> (dark it is)
>> dark

>> as penumbra of the echo
>> of the darkest big brass gong

shadow
>> of the discus thrower
>> as he leans and hurls

clong
>> of the big bass drum
>> of a Storyville dirge
>> dinging out of b & w raceflick

privation
>> of sun collapsing
>> into its own cavity but

also access
>> ibility of all light
>> from antipodal solstices

solace
>> of the dark epic, alliterative

ode and meticulous assonance

also agi
            tation of the fierce lum
            inosity, many-tongued

    song
            of the deepest abstraction
            edging toward hierarchic spec

    ificity
            Yeats' gong
            gooonnggs goes

            gongon

likesound
            jutting out toward its own
            border, yet clong

            ing itself darkly in its own
            sources

            that disc

us   of
                        sound that
        sharp
                ness that
                        surge

of the gong as it pierces
                    into Night cast

ing its vast shadow-light

where Dawn echoes on domed steeples and equal altars
of serenity.

That thin

mechanic air
bringing Thomas Hardy
such heidde

gerian Care
across the thresh
hold of a century

now swirls
at my door gob
lets of silence

never quite
amesh
tiny gongs of crystal

articulation, coring
ajar reticent sparks
of renunciation

hov
              er

                              ov

er sycamore and porch,
air of resig
nation, swirl

ing in the very
midst of blighted
headstones—thin

mechanic tint touch

ing the cheeks of
that country blonde

holding a lamp in the
casement. then
that air

tracing the tint
of a century
brings the scent

of Thomas Hardy's
carriage
(hooves and horsefart)

moving in stir
ruped hei
ddegerean rhythm

on dusty battered
wessex roads
balding mustached british

poet
in the vested suit
starched white collar.

come
festering through the brok
en carriage windows

finch and thrush, brash
starling, fractious
jay, dove and

cuckoo—all manner
of creatures
that squawk and squeak

and thunk and thirl and thud

O Thomas thom
        as
              hardyger   that

        thin mech
               an

                      ic

                              air!

Hugh
Fox
(1932 -)

*Achieves universality through the representation
of personal experiences combined with
public/cultural images, to present the poet
as a metaphor for everyman. His work attempts
to break through barriers of personal
inhibition & psycho-social preconceptions.*

from Guernica Cycle

July 5, 1976, Monday - Valencia, Spain

Mighty Mouse Goes On Her Travels

"She won't remember anything."
everyone says,
and she *doesn't* know whether
she's in Michigan, Mexico or
Madrid,
first-speaks equally in
Spanish and English
but she sees lion-faces on door-knockers,
angel-faces on drainpipes,
a red woven skirt on an
oporto doll,
an 18th-century tile-
bordered mirror or a
gold spike-haloed figure
of the Virgin of the Losers
(*desamparados*) dispensing
her Grace over a lost
candle-lit crowd,
sees fountains and marble-shod
plazas, a hedge of oleanders,
a mosaic statue of Donald
Duck,
and can sit through the
whole of *Singing in the Rain*
(Spanish dub-in except for
the songs)
without even flinching.

August 16, 1976, Monday - London

Depressed by thoughts of going back...I went to Salder's Wells again tonight to see the Harlem Dance Theater and got there about an hour early, walked around Islington and the area around the theater, visited a Victorian church called St. Marks, this one square which had obviously been up HIGH during the Victorian times and then sunk LOW some years ago, is being refurbished; renovated now, all nice brass doorknockers on the handles of the big front doors (I think the name of the street was Myddleton, the church St. Mark's of Pentonville), dreaming up a novel about drought and the fact that Salder's Wells is built on wells and the TWA (Thames Water Authority) is right next to Salder's Wells, and I look up and see a River Street...my novel about London in its 44th year of drought, one third of the population has died, all the parks are a desert, there's no money to buy fuel for the desalination plants, a dictator arises who lives in this secret underground waterworld in Islington ("Isl" like from "Isle"), and his name is Tlaloc (the same as the Aztec watergod) and...well, I was half-way between Wells-Lovecraft and thinking "Gees, I wonder how much a house around here would cost?" Saw a Church of England girl's school down the road, thought "Marg and Alexandra could go to school here...," the very thought of going back to East Lansing depresses the shit out of me - the Great Vacuum.

The whole day *sang* today, Haymarket (American Express), then Charing Cross, down to the river, fish and chips, which we ate in the Victoria Embankment Gardens listening to a 1940's Big Band concert, then through the gardens, slow, let the kids enjoy it, lots of statues (Robert Burns, a monument to the Camel Corps, Cleopatra's Needle, a statue of Arthur Sullivan being mourned by a muse) over to the Temple, the temple Church just closing (KNIGHTS TEMPLARS - hence the name...12th century...now it's all law offices), down Fleet Street to Doctor Johnson's House, over to Old Bailey, Nona went on with Margaret to this religious bookstore in Pater Noster

40

Square (St. Paul's), Alexandra and I just bummed along, I bought her an ice cream which she devoured meticulously, then we went over to St. Paul's she wanted Mama, I pointed up to the big dome, "Is that Mama?", "Yes", she shook her head, yes. She's such a HEAD, the dome of St. Paul's is her mother.

from Apotheosis of Olde Towne

We begin with UNITY,

> green space
> green eye
> green mind,

LAZA
P IAZZA
  ACE
  AVILLION

> playspace,

> > eye to eye under glass grass,

wayspace,
    chess,
      chat,
    color upflung - pipe in birds!

The Stock Exchange Building facade,

expanded
exaggerated
brought to its limit

then passed
new limits created
then passed, past them again
limits after limits after limits...

THE EXECUTION OF JOHN S. VAN BERGER,
HUBERT AND DANIEL (Jr.) BURNHAM,
IRVING AND ALLEN POND

     and company.

Guilty
of
the
STONE
Q
U
A
R
E LINE!!!

    The Golden Schmalt Door of the
    Transportation Building (1893),
      The vault over the orchestra floor of
        The Theater in the Schilb Building
        (1891-92)

We begin with UNITY,
        green,
the curved eye and the curved mind.

from **Back**

Back, back, back, always coming back to the white walls
  and

42

the red roofs, stands of bamboo in the bloody afternoon
    light,
floresta, eucalyptus,   the blessed poor hills, the smell of
    burning
(incensed) wood, Siva dancing on the hills,   plumed
    serpent red
in the midst of a circle of lotus, the old gods here, hidden,
    donkey
carts and cripples, in the beginning were the (green) hills
    and winged
spirits, another summit. another lagoon, bloodclot earth,
    the cosmic
dance goes on, I wrap serpents around my neck and find
    the highest
untouched summit and begin (*einmal, nur einmal und
    nichts mehr /*
once and only once and no more) to unpleat, expand
    brotar / sprout.
spread wings, never realizing until after you've lost it
    where/what
you (never can be again)
were.

17.
Everything changing, at the same time always the same,
interchangeable black suede heels and shocks of blonde
hair,
idiomas glissando, uno con otro / languages sliding, one
with the other,
Aztec *Papalo,* French *Papillon,*
vieux, velho, veijo, veccio,
arrowing back to the latino time of
old,
old,
old
Caesar.

43

18.

A little *ayahuasca* and the walls begin to melt
and what was always there is finally there,
you think your eyes see and your ears hear,
as if the universe of your limited electromagnetic
spectrum was the universe, as if it all were measurable
wavelengths already known and catalogued.

Terrible Angels

The prince, Prince Johannes Von Thurm und Taxis, is
very gracious as he invites us into his favorite salon filled with
snuffboxes displayed in quietly illuminated, glass-covered
tables.

"This one's worth two and a half million," says the
prince handing me a snuffbox made out of dark green jasper
and richly decorated with flowers made out of diamond,
emerald, rubies and a potpourri of semi-precious stones..."

"Beautiful," I say.

Chris isn't too impressed. All the footmen and waiters
and maids and bodyguard-chauffers and the three-hundred
and fifty rooms of the Schloss (castle) St. Emmeram don't
(wouldn't) impress him. I can hear his mind thinking, "Where's
the video games?"

"Rulers used to exchange snuffboxes as tokens of
appreciation when they made a visit, or in appreciation for
something else. Like this one was given to one of my ancestors
by Frederick the Great..."

"Great!" I say, and the Princess Maria Gloria Ferdinana
Joachima Josephine Wilhelmine Huberta, the prince's wife,
comes in and invites us to take a little tour.

We go to the library filled with paintings of Christ, King
of Heaven and Christ Crucified, he shows us first editions of

Lully's *Alceste* signed by Louis XIV, the *Pastoralis Cura* of St. Gregory the Great dating from 1120 and so forth, and then on to see snuffboxes and commodes, Meissen clocks and figures, Japanese lacquer cabinets, silver candleabrum, 480 rare and priceless clocks, mechanical birds, endless rooms covered with room-sized paintings...

The prince never stops talking.

"You might find it interesting as to how we got the name Thurm und Taxis. It begins as Tasso, the first Tassos were robbers, then became 'protectors' against robbers, then started protecting 'things', a mail service began...in the fifteenth century the family acquired a castle with a tower and the name acquired a Tarriani which become della Torre e Tasso... the ones who moved north to the Holy Roman Empire changed Torre to Thurm, and Tasso to Taxis...hence Thurm und Taxis..."

"Fascinating," I say as we sit down in the Baroque dining room for a little meringues glacées avec friandises and some coffee, "I do have one question...your mother, I believe, lent Rilke one of your castles and that's where he wrote the *Duino Elegies...*'

"You open old wounds," he says, "It wasn't this castle...in fact the castle that Rilke wrote the *Duino Elegies* in was destroyed during the Second World War...it's an obliterated chapter in world literary history..."

"Not necessarily," says Chris and pulls a tall conical hat out of his pocket and sticks it atop his head, "grab hands, I'll show you a trick...*Es ist Zeit für die Hexe zu arbeiten...*," which I understand, "It is time for the witch to work." He must have heard it during last winter's *Hansel und Gretel*.

We join hands and off we go, the faint sound of music in the air - Mahler's *First*. You don't have to go any further. Off and up into the dark, cold but somehow beyond cold, an ethereal, etherized cold, the cold of dreams and little deaths, over forests and towns, smoke stacks and little huts, the forests in which the Brothers Grimm collected their fairy tales, up to a mountain still filled with giant black blocks of former castle walls.

"It looks like Dracula's castle," I say.

"The *Duino Elegies* castle," whispers the prince in hushed reverence.

And we touch down, a small man in a dark wool coat there in front of us in the moonlight, kneeling down, his face full up into the salt-white mucosal light, an Angel coming down on the escalator moonbeam like right out of *Hansel und Gretel*, the Angel speaking, over and over again the same thing, Rilke, the small man in the dark wool coat, it must be, listening, crying:

> Wir haben nur einmal,
> Einmal gewesen zu sein, nicht
> Mehr, nur einmal und nichts meht...

> We have only once,
> Once to be, not
> more, only once and not more...

from The Year Book

III.

My ghosts with me full time all day today, and not just
my personal ghosts but the hordes coming out of India,
Africa, into Asia Minor, Assyria, Tiawanaku, the northern
Columbian coast, always searching, searching, searching for
gods (that they'd invent), rituals to cope with the whole
mystere of the Out There that surrounded them, never
ever getting used to Winter into Summer in a week, that
sudden shift into almost total green that turns my old
Victorian neighborhood almost spanking new, you don't
see the shabby roof or windows or unpainted column on the

46

front porch, it's just all old trees and new tulips, Ed
    Recchia
and, you know, the guy who lived on health food, Reed
    Baird, both
brain cancer, Todd Moore, AIDS, Ted Erlandson an
    esophageal
hernia that ruptured, Frank Sullivan cancer, Father Surtz, a
    car
hit him on his bicycle when he was down in Tampa on a
    vacation...
falling in love with my two hundred year old house,
    wanting it to
talk, wanting ghosts, wanting to be a ghost myself forever and
    forever
up this chimney, inside these walls, in the leaded glass and
    marble
fireplace, Armour, Swift, Banrum (as in Barnum and
    Bailey), up the
Hudson, Prairie Avenue (Chicago), imitating king, count,
    lord...and
then joining them in oblivion.

from The Book of Ancient
Revelations

I can see the desert suddenly spring to life again, a new
Eden spread out in what today is sand, using the latest solar-
energy techniques for energy, using the rivers that are nearby,
using the snow that covers the craters of the extinct volcanoes,
returning to how it was before "The Fall", to its original Edenic
state.

We know why, in so many Assyrian and Sumerian
seals, we find the king twinned, flanking a strange tree filled
with mysterious fruit, with the Sun hovering directly above it,
and a birdman behind the king, with something in one hand, in

47

what looks like the act of handing something to the king.

The Sun directly above the tree is the Sun at the moment of the winter solstice, the tree itself, of Good and Evil, of Knowledge, is the psychedelic tree of enlightenment, and the king, twinned like the Morning and Evening Stars that accompany the Sun through the solar year, is about to eat the forbidden fruit and be taken aloft by the birdman familiar...

We are at the theophanic moment of enlightenment, the passage into godhead.

Is it by accident that Har Karkom, the mountain where Moses received the ten commandments from God, is to this day filled with psychedelic plants?

We dwell in the cities of madness, the jails overloaded with God-seeing criminals who are seeking the divine using the wrong drugs in the wrong places in all the wrong ways. All the "Indians" in the Andes, the descendants of the sacred, ancient races from the Mediterranean, the Indus Valley, and the Middle East, chew coca from childhood until tranquil old age. But we have perverted coca and turned it into the killer drug for The Lost who really seeking the Tree of God, the Tree of the Garden of Eden, the fruit that makes old men young again, that opens the mind and spirit, that opens the door into the horizon of enhanced, superior knowledge, unblocks perception and makes enlightened intuitiveness a part of the everyday workings of the mind, the fruit that was converted by The Ancients into a goddess! Peyote. San Pedro cactus...or any of a wide variety of cacti, vines, mushrooms, which are all the flesh of the gods that (in the proper setting of Old Eden) accompanied by appropriate rites and rituals, turn mortals into gods, open the doors of perception so that we see with the brain as well as the eyes...

I see the Desert of Eden, the Solstice Point, repopulated, and at the center of each community a Chapel of Communication, and in the center of the chapel, a tabernacle housing the Apples of Immortality/Enlightenment, the whole communal life centered around the ebb and flow of the seasons, the points of the solar year's configurations, solstices and equinoxes...

...on the day of the winter solstice itself, I see the vast plains that surround Tiawanaku, the holy city, the Home of the Gods, filled with the Enlightened Ones, waiting in the pre-dawn for the ever-dying, ever-renewing Sun to rise, the high priest of enlightenment atop the Akapana temple, crying out, the Muezzin of the Dawn, "NOW!" The Sun rises up as it always has and always will, until the end of time, up above Mount Illimani, the Chinese Mount Kunlun, across our sacred world, the Chinese Land of the Washu (our Wanaku). At high noon, millions of pilgrims on the great plain of Tiawanaku, take the sacred drug, and as the Sun descends over Titicaca/Thunder Lake, it becomes, once again, the Plumed Serpent, Lord Thunder, bird and snake, earth and sky, Ego and Id, the holistic reunification of our split and fragmented psychic forces, so that a giant cry reaches out from the assembled Hassidim: "*Inti, King Sun, Lord of the Year, has returned.*"

The Ancients were in contact with the gods, could talk to the animals, felt at *one* with the universe. Now we can return to The Center and reopen the pathways to the "forces" that surround us in Nature. We are no longer severed from our connection to the Anima Mundi, the Spirit of the World, but live inside the Omega Point of contact between humanity and the divine, where geography matches psychology and mind-chemistry is properly realigned with the currents of universal being that flow around us and through us, but which are usually invisible to everyone but the "initiated".

Now we are *all* initiated, we are a society of holy shamans whose center is the sacred, expanded, ordered, rhythmic NOW.

Começar de Novo/Beginning Again

6.
I let it all rush in, Praia do Forte,
the galleons and the first Conquistadores,
the sunken continents of old images reappear,
stained with the breath of the tides the wind of
night comes in, we are dogs and ferrets, owls
and anacondas, our metaphysics the smell of
night and the sounds of beetles in the leaves

8.
Walking through the flowering crabapple, magnolia, yellow
  wood,
cherry forests, the ground littered with magenta, carmine,
  pink-white
snow, the ferns unfurling, the ground all sprouting with
  first and second
and then third-sprouts that finally proclaim genus and
  species,
under the scudding tornado-watch clouds, rain and sun,
  sun and rain,
sparse beginning lavender and the spread of thyme, the
  green sliced-
paper fingers of orris root, bushy hyssop, belligerent terry
  box,
triumphant cow parsnip, maidenhair fern, hop and
  hydrangea,
blaring meadow saffron and the sunshot exuberance of
  choctaw
root...this is the time of renaming, Old Fire Grandfather in
  the middle
and the Regents at the four solstice Quarters, became all
  that we were
charged to be, rising from the rim of the forty thousand
  foot

horizon, filling the windows of our eyes with the stellar furnace light
of all our possible futures, shaped from the eclecticism of all our possible pasts.

from Shin Ku Myo U, The Sixties and Me

The first step toward Sixties Zen was a radical "reductionism" - a stepping outside of the mechanistic opulence of the twentieth century into an interiorized prehistory...

I moved to California...in 1958 and spent huge chunks of time in San Francisco/Berkeley with my cousin, Jim McNitt, who was getting his Ph.D. in Geology from the University of California in Berkeley.

I'd go out early into Golden Gate Park and see the mystics playing flutes up in the midst of the trees, or bundled in mummy-bundle sleeping bags on the grass. I'd go visit my friends, the Cochrans, on Portrero Hill, and we'd sit bundled in blankets ourselves, watching the fog roll in across the hills like shaving cream or toothpaste, until it finally got to us and buried us.

The other side of the coin, of course, was Wondrous Being, but that could only come after The Great Negation, something like St. John of the Cross' VIA NEGATIVE/NEGATIVE WAY.

The music (I'm thinking of Country Joe and the Fish) was mantric. Sometimes it would actually be the deep, guttural, sound-intoning of Tibetan Buddhism. And it would put up its hands and stop Technological-Industrial Time.

The clock stopped. Even went backwards.

I remember Julie down in Chinatown going around shoeless, just tights, big runs up her legs, getting on those mechanical horses that you put a penny in (now a quarter), or just walking around *looking, looking, looking*.

I remember myself down in New Orleans, after a poetry reading with Bruchac at the Jerusalem Gardens, finding myself in the top of this apartment in a book warehouse, finding a bed and staring for hours at the beaded red curtain.

That was the key to the psychedelic - to turn The Real into a Psychic Delicatessen.

That's the way D.A. Levy's apartment was in Cleveland - every inch of the ceiling painted in psychedelic patterns.

He was forever writing of the Quiet Place (in *The North American Book of the Dead*), riding a white horse (Heroin) to the Quiet Place out of the World's Noise.

The Amerindians had Peyote and Magic Mushrooms and a thousand other mind-altering drugs...the Hindus had Datura..Moses' mountain in Israel is filled with narcotic, mind-altering drug-plants. What really happened when Moses received The Ten Commandments?

We were all convinced that "unaltered" Reality wasn't Reality at all, but only a grey film that covered the splendour within creation. We all wanted to see The Gods/The Godliness of Creation Itself.

I remember Charlie Potts/Laffing Water in Berkeley when he was writing *Little Lord Shiva*, looking down at the toilet bowl when he was taking a piss and seeing it a millions miles away. No wonder the cover of *Little Lord Shiva* is of a giant Potts walking across the surface of the moon. That's where we all walked all the time - the moon's surface, between the stars.

We had rediscovered the paleolithic, put our hands up against the cave-surface of the reality that surrounded us and blown charcoal around the edges so we could leave our imprint on Eternity.

Like the Queche Indians in Ecuador, we took The Sacred Drug (in their case boiled-down, concentrated tobacco) and waited for the appearance of The Great Snake. We wore The Great Snake draped around our necks. We became The Great Snake ourselves, Ananta, The Eternity Serpent, Vishnu seated upon our coils, dreaming his universe-creating dreams.

52

The Western World represented an abrasive tick-tock of technological assembly-line time; the Mystic Eastern World that we aspired to was a continuous hum, bamboo brush-strokes across The Great Void.

I remember my first wife, Lucia Ungaro de Zevallos, the Peruvian poet, in Levy's apartment in Cleveland. Besides the psychedelic walls, the whole place was filled with statues of Siva in the Cosmic Fire-Ring, Mandalas, Yamas...

"Have you ever been to India?" she asked.

"No," he answered, heroin-pale skin, tortured eyes, black beard and hair. I remember the Siamese cats playing in the sunlight on the floor. "I've never been out of Cleveland."

Which was the point, wasn't it? Cleveland was India. India was inside you. You became India.

In 1964-66 I spent two years in Caracas and then lectured throughout Bolivia, Chile, Peru...I had already learned how to open myself up to the Divine Moment, open the doors not merely of perception, but on an epistemological plane, open the doors of being, so that I merged with the green, with the rivers, the ruins, the ideologies, Intihuatana, Where the Sun is Tied, Machu Picchu with the clouds forming in the Urubamba Valley and coming up like chiffon scarves across my face as I looked down from the stone parapets...

"All day long showering..."

All day long showering myself with Bruckner, Richard
Strauss, Schönberg, Mahler, and then at night, the only
lights on up in the 35 foot ceiling, the voices coming
in from the dark garden, "Prague, Vienna, Budapest...
what are you doing here...no rivers, cafes, cymbals, *Ich liebe
dich, wie du liebst mich...Lieder eines fahrenden Gesellen...
Die zwei blauen Augen.*, here take my hand," coming in
through the glass, I take it and step out into the garden,
"Of course you know you'll never come back..."

The House

Everyone else asleep, my
spirit walks back to the
house in La Paz, Bolivia, the GREATEST
time, the kitchen, tiled
floor and tiled boveada
ceiling, surprise corridors
and eccentric stairways,
the texture of walls and
floors, the texture of sun
through prismatic windows, I
see myself as an old man in
an old house, but the texture
of the house is important as
all textures have always been
important, why did I spend so
many years negating the **texture**
of the moon on the backyard
leaves, the texture of Sunday
morning on her interested
face?

Bienestar/Well-Being

Light tree blowing
out of the negative
projective night wind
soil, embryo dream
finger unlocking the
endocrine doors of
day

Beating Around the Bush

Im wunderschönen Monat Mai / In the
wonderful month of May,
back a hundred + years in Grand Ledge,
but it could be Stuttgart, Prague, Budapest,
Wien/Vienna, soaked in Hapsburgian peace,
everything balconies and attention to roofs
and cobblestones, the right sausages with
the right sauerkraut - *bier* /beer, *Ich Grolle
nicht!* / I bear no grudge,
against war every day in the air like exhaust
fumes from a truck that needs fixing, but
Die Rose, die Lillie, die Taube, die Sonne /
The rose, the lily, the dove, the sun,
vibrate so much fuller
when you think there'll be a
tomorrow.

from The Fourteenth, The Greatest of Centuries

There it was. 1511 Dearborn Parkway. 1511 was the year that Michelangelo painted the sibyls in the Sistine Chapel.

The fourteenth, the greatest of centuries. The 16th seemed so "late" for him now. So..."fleshy". So renaissance-ish. As in re-nascer. To be reborn. Only what was being reborn was the "fleshiness" of the Bacchus-Dionysius Graeco-Roman world. Where he really felt at home was right in the middle of the fourteenth century, where flesh was still rigid, eyes staring, frozen...Byzantine, The Empress Theodora. Frozen, immortal Christ, Dante's Beatrice:

Oltre la spera che piu larga gira
passa 'Isospiro ch'esce del mio core:
intelligenzia nova, che l'Amore
piangendo mette in lui...

Beyond the sphere what makes a larger turn
passes the sigh arisen from my heart:
a new intelligence, that Love, weeping,
placed in him.

Kevin was Dante and Petra, Beatrice. It wasn't Chicago, 1953, but Florence, 1353, maybe not even Florence but some point in Neo-Platonic-Augustinian hyperspace where you weren't in your body at all but just pure soul in the heaven of the Mystical Rose:

> per che tornar con gli occhi a Beatrice
> ...la bellezza ch'io vidi si transmoda
> non pur di la da noi, ma certo io credo
> che solo il suo fattor tutta la goda.

> I turned my eyes toward Beatrice
> ...the beauty that I saw, transcending measure,
> goes not only beyond our reach, but I believe
> can only be totally enjoyed by the Maker himself.

He didn't want to park on Dearborn Parkway at all. After all, he was almost an hour early, what if someone might be looking out the window by chance. "How come you always come an hour early?"

Good question - how come he always DID come an hour early?

Slid around the corner over to State Parkway, found a spot by the curb, got out and put on his top coat. All tweed, imitation grey Harris tweed suit with matching vest, now his grey tweed topcoat, homburg on his head. Even if he wasn't in a Dantean-Platonic netherworld, he certainly wasn't in hog-butcher of the world Chicago just a few years after World War II either!

He was reading Aldous Huxley's *Point Counter Point* for the umpteenth time and State Parkway reminded him of Huxley's London...again the undefinable aura of wealth...mews, coach houses, brass railings and doorknobs, rounded bay windows veiled in curtains and drapes through which you looked into high-ceilinged living rooms full of stately lamps, stolid furniture and new TV's, basement steps that led into plush leather apartments...

A cold gust of north wind and he wrapped his muffler around his neck, held on to his homburg.

He was thin to the point of emaciation, mainly because he forgot to eat. And fasting was so intimate a part of his routine that food, flesh, fat, seemed almost evil.

Evil versus Good.

St. Augustine.

Manicheanism.

Light versus Darkness.

And the People of Light were always thin, "controlled", like St. Augustine controlling his eyes, controlling the subterranean movements of his mind.

Why did The Word (**Verbum**) ever (**Incarnatus Est**) become Flesh, why didn't it (he) just stay Word.

The gutters and lawns already filled with fallen leaves. *Oh, Wild West Wind, breath of Autumn's being...*

Lights going on now, each house like a massive stone ship, a kingdom unto itself...

...there was something very ethereal about her, Raphael, Giotto, or even earlier, a mosaic Empress Theodora, a coptic portrait that straddled the line between abstraction and real flesh and blood:

Oh quanto e corto il dire e como fioco al mio concetto! / Oh how lacking the language and how to frame my thoughts!

from Techniques

5.
The old bricks calling me to come back, this is where
I was born, my ghosts still inside the stone waiting
for my touch to be reborn and come back into the sullen
wind of the living world.

23.
The snow begins to melt, I walk over to the Newberry
Library, new street sign, Ruth Page Street, her ballet legs
suddenly in front of me, I was 10, 12, hanging around
backstage in the wings at the Civic Opera House, like
having read Villon, Catallus, Martial, having sat listening
to Gagaku in the court of the Shogun in seventeenth
century Kyoto.

26.
In Marshall Fields, a woman with her two
daughters speaking Czech, holding up a
dress, I pass by and offer an opinion, "*Krazny/*
beautiful," she agrees, the woman in the shoestore
Italian, raised in French-speaking Switzerland, but
we talk English, at lunch I slip into Spanish with the
waiter who feels awkward in English, a Coptic Egyptian
next to me at Border's (for lunch), a Yoruba (Nigerian) cab-
driver on the way to the Art Institute, no one melting into
anyone else, another wave always coming in, Chicago
always seen as refuge, opening, hope, renewal, unchange
within change.

36.
Mahler's *Fifth*, after three movements
of irritating fragments suddenly it comes
together in the Adagietto, the smooth flow
of black Viennese lines in the diasporic
air, all these faces around me, the wrinkled
old Jewish lady next to me with the ridiculous
rabbit fur hat strapped to the top of her head
under her chin with a white elastic band,
the Polish-Czech face of the girl who came in
late standing up over in the corner, we come
into and leave the garden alone, between
the coming and the going a few attempted
moments of surrender amidst the distrustful
sprouting-falling leaves

Nocturne in Blue and Silver

Childe Hassam 110 years
ago painting the edge of
the Boston Commons, so
many of the buildings the same,
the little girls in the picture would
be 114, 115, 116 now, their
parents 150, 151, 152, a white-
haired old lady notices me
writing, vanishes into the next gallery.

59

from **Eternity**

14.
Old street lights, red brick
apartment houses a hundred
plus years old, I can't see the
river but only the decline of
the line toward it, cars rushing
by, all through white muslin curtains.

15.
Words hardly do it, the pigeons
sailing off the top of
the red brick warehouse
in the oblique almost-winter
late afternoon sun, white
ceramic tile, green-painted
steel/copper cornices and
balustrades, one apartment
house with the west side
curved all the way down,
probably living rooms,
Margaret 25, Rebecca 3
months, Bernadete 49, Chris
16, me 66, the nineteenth,
twentieth and twenty-first
centuries closing in
around me.

Kirby Congdon

(1924 -   )

*Combines neo-classical musical elements with
contemporary language & imagistic detail,
to evoke recognition of existential truths.*

The Lot

We walked our parallels
in trolley tracks through wood
where rails unwound in weeds
and rusty goldenrod.
Yellow, shattering tree trunk shadows,
flashed in the far electric hum.

Fountains of gladioli rose to my father's hand,
his shoulders brown above the prim-leaved plants.
His hat, a worn-out sun, hid his head,
his mouth, past pain or praise.
On that hot day, one comfort came:
water, wet and tinted green in jugs
propped in jungles of honeysuckle caves.
The first drops bounced in dust
of that summer day's-end rain
before the long hike back
to the streets of town
and the poplar's thin shade.

The rails were steel and straight.
Clouds had curdled before the storm.
Evening was gray, grave.

Rowboats

With an apple orchard off to starboard
blooming blossoms in an apple cloud,
in a boat, stored, forgotten,
like a pagan pyre for a burial mound,
piled with pears, and drunk with wonder,
under grapes whose arbor's vines

were complex riggings
for a leafy sail,
I rowed,
as to some out-of-season's final harvest,
past the peak of the high house eaves,
beyond the looming shadow of the cliff-like barn
and left behind the chicken run
and the flowering fruits of a kitchen garden,
like islands, so civilized! but dismissed
by an easy child's lone abandon.
Swamped by years of leaves' debris,
the bilge awash, though rooted
with the seedlings of tiny weeds
like green leaks seeping, secret,
in between the stove-in hull's split seams,
and with a meadow's wake of Queen Anne's lace,
the rowboat's rotten hulk,
in such dubious comforts, carried one
through each day's drifting span
when the sun's daily sway,
standing still in childhood's time,
stopped and, immobile, stayed
any change of sea of whatever kind
as if my brief, broken craft
were only made for sounding out
the chartless map of a summer's edge
among the dangerous shoals ahead.
But when the burden of the body
and its heavy bones are also gone,
my own body's boat shall likewise float
as my spine's keel rides
its own calm oceans, prone,
in prim, sedate repose.
The prow holds on
to its ancient course
though my sea, now dry, is dust

and my ballast: the whole world's single stone,
as that earth itself carries out
all our history's weight
through the galactic spirals
of reeling light
that, dipping, spin
and, leaning, tilt
in wild career,
like derelicts drunk
on the dizzy spill
of the shifting sky's lurching lilt
like a song one's heard before,
out of time, out of place,
wheeling round inside one's mind
titleless, tuneless and uncomposed.
Even now the waves of stars
rise or fall in their swirling tide.
Their furrows, forked before my bow,
blow their spray across the rise
of the final dark.
And if I insist and take a look,
the salty sense of the commonplace
would sting lids shut to spare surprise
in the last sights spied,
shattering the light of what I'd seen
in the wide round compass
of my dazzled eyes.

Tank Driver

The back roads straight,
each hill laid low,
the thickets split,
saplings bent, splintered, broke,
and before my track
each boundary fell.

The clanking tread and engine roar
of my mechanic love
made earth's rim shake.
And in the grip
of white-knuckled fists,
my shoulders, back, and arms
were charged,
and waged their wars.
Though no war's won,
I ran earth down,
and by manoeuvres learned
the ponderous skills
of crawling
a turtle's
slow terrain.
So I, and my age, continued on.

That heavy hulk must be rusting now,
the hard steel guts of those white insides,
pitted with the ulcerous indigestions of decay,
the armored shell, the one-eyed cannon's bore,
blind, dismantled or melted down.
But the squeaking ghost
of that great machine lumbers on.

A universe of dust,
thick from a hot exhaust,
still hangs on air
and the clatter of a day,
long gone, reappears
as the steady crush
of earth's iron wheel,
through each tense of my affection,
also
charges
on.

Ego

If enemies amputate
both hands and arms,
I still walk
across a summer ground,
and, legless, I can see
the world revolve.
Blind, my mouth will sing
beyond my eyes.
Tongue torn out,
I shall hear
the season turn.
When I am deaf
to my own cries,
and the visions
in my own mind chill,
this heart will beat
like the world's own clock.
And when for want of winding
the works run down,
no man dies:
it's the world that stops.

Victory Song

After cheers, the season's game,
and the home-town team
in their parade,
I saw on porches, around the square,
the sun's own heart
cast a slant, though fading,
of our last light
along a door before the dark
where some facade

had caught a spark.
But still the celebrations lit the clouds
and split the roof of that booming sky
as, underneath, each street filled up,
bright, it seemed, with our distant cries
though even earth's own shadow
turned and began to rise,
mourning for any town's demise;
even lovers, lying tidy
in their single sheets below the ground
cease to writhe in their last delights,
suspended, as it were, from the glories won
in their exercise when desire
still survived its prostrate fate,
like that of all our own hard-won lives.
Even ashes, like another truth,
dry all our ripened colors out,
in the failures of a fallen sun.
That trash itself was once on fire
when all the different arms we knew
beckoned us, as Horace said,
in the city dusk to be led,
easy, beyond desire.
In such unions, even still,
we separate our private ends
from all the public's current dead
and wait, now or then
for a hand, at last! to come
and feed our frenzy
where greedy roots, in any dust,
seek to have their passions fed
in the dark remove
of a private room
on a passing lover's
blazing bed.

I Walk on Sand

I walk on sand
and leave a trail
of footprints, hard and deep.
The wash of waves
fills my step
in hasty cascades.
Water and sand return,
not quite the same;
the tide, its oceans,
the earth itself
are changed.

The High Diver

makes a sport of those deadly heights,
does tricks as he dies,
discards the body's bones,
an offering, neatly in order,
in rite's form, for their final fall
where our formal histories began.
Silence supports the arrested air,
sustains its movement by his heels,
then violence boils underwater
around his ears,
with suicides of applause.
There, he and his body,
gone to another water's world,
proud, though almost sad,
are a smaller majesty
in the weather's air
of this burning atmosphere's

circular blaze – from birth to death,
from his skill's private practice,
to the public's practiced praise.
By his naked body, we are adorned;
and in such a dying, are born.

Discus Thrower

The discus thrower puts his body's weight
behind the power sprung in his engine's arms,
unspins, in his twisting spring, an unspent fury,
unjust neglect, pent-up sorrow, an old regret
like some dead loss
in the hard weight of his iron disc,
a hate he can't forget
propelled against the pull
of this sullen world's slow turning.
Stopping time, arresting change,
his instance delineates
the clear, true line
of each dimension's depth,
in one complete moment's flight
from where he stands
and, so, extends himself
as idea tears, ideal,
through the insubstantial air
and races to the far, hard corners
of absolute matter's uncertain space.

His figure, cut in silhouette
with no excess expended
nor stint in measure,
takes its careful aim.
But his body's torso, used,
in the practice of his art,

without want or waste,
is its own long-distance mark,
a record made for an afternoon
- as marble shapes
engraved against the air
make the centuries halt
and stand in wait
to score a time upon an age
as if forever
like humankind
against the fates.

Boiled Egg

By habit's ritual,
ceremonial attitude,
death's ban shatters,
the bird's germ dead,
masticated, digested.
Spoon, cup, egg -
pomp is practical
and mitigates predicaments.
The daily mass of manners
- a requiem for the dying
of some good thing
whose death sustains us -
completes the ruin
whose continual form
revolves around us.
Only the thin-skinned
have hard shells against it
and avoid the oval,
or devious and oblique.
In a square room
with cup and spoon

I make no prayer for the dead;
horror into manner,
I, by ceremony,
like wine or wafer,
daily dying,
pray for me
and eat the egg.

Brooklyn Poem

It's a cold day in hell
and even "dog-do" at every step
is frozen white on the sidewalks.
Legless men sit without motion,
almost formless in the morning shadows
in their chrome-plated wheel chairs,
waiting for the silver disk of the sun
to slide past the corners
of the historical buildings.
Even the children are cowed,
without tears, without power,
beaten down - at last - into their first silence.
The alley cats are gone,
nor do even cat lovers care.
The frantic hearts of the cold automobiles
gasp in starts against the glossy air
to churn over their little lives of perpetual bliss.
The trolley tracks are choked with tar
and the frozen steel shines,
ruler-straight, like an old grief,
polished, remembered,
but without use.
Motorcycles, cradled down
in their stiff tarpaulins,
ride their reckless dreams,

their antlers tilted like listeners
for news of the impossible.
Iron gates - of the garden yards,
the abandoned vestibules of the mansions,
the store-front windows of dark shops,
across the subway entrances,
and at the ticket windows -
are closed, their padlocks shut
where Orpheus has gone crazy.
But in my mind warm melodies
hurry, though tuneless and numb,
to my mute lips,
where they float and dissipate
in clouds of open harmony,
like the slow ghost of an explosion.
Those songs set a delicate fire
to the blazing mist of my breath.
Their solar storms enlarge
and celebrate the glory of the dead
with the grey, rising chorus
of a million deaf angels.

Jack Hammer

Shuddering lid,
stuttering tongue,
tattoo-twitch
iterate the tic
of pneumatic drills.
Cement cracks
as the one-toothed bit bites,
and gets to the heart of the matter
hidden under hard pavement.
And that needle sews
no seams across this broken rock,

73

but would rather jar
the earth itself
into a shaking mass
of mud and water
- or whatever single-minded passion
that joy in rage
must be lusting after.

Steam Shovel

The mind mad, its skull stripped
of flesh and indecision,
the voice reduced to banging bark
from jawbones hinged to the guttling maw,
the steam shovel, dry, vomits stone;
the howling engines wretch
and disgorge the innards of the earth
onto the staggering backs of trucks
as a butcher weighs clumps of viscera
on the platforms of scales.
The machine grovels to eat the living rock
its own treads stand on,
passion deeper than the gutters of the street,
and sinks, stiff-necked and chin-deep,
into the sure, certain sewers
of its own self-righteous pit.

Effigy in Snow
(*Homage to Leonard Baskin*)

Stolid in the old reproof
of faith betrayed,
denying even death's thin bones,
another Niobe stands

in a constant flood's decay.
The face, lost, its color drained,
the skull's lump, numb with cold,
are witness to each passing age,
even now our own.
In hell, her melting body's gestures burn.
Of stone, of snow, she wears the white
of each stark funeral's dress.
The voice speechless
before such dead parades
as her kind has known,
the mouth alone, though mute, out-cries
the whole of silence in its lament.
So she sings though stripped of song.
And the blank sockets,
so blurred at each black surprise,
bear coals as hard as cinders
in depressions for the eyes.
And if the eyes, crazed, are both gone wrong,
she sees beyond the wash of our pale day.
And when the darkness comes,
large across the town,
her figure stands, and in all that black,
- though blind - her two dark eyes
stare
night
down.

Key West Cemetery

Under lonely festivals
of the blown-up moon,
staggering with its weightless space
in the ripe blackness
of the blooming night's perfume,

their strict bodies lie
between the frozen sheets
drawn, single, over stony beds,
tilted, reckless in their abandon,
pitched about in the old decay
of their common room,
where marbleized cement secures in paint
the white repose, though mottled,
like a spotted innocence,
and fake flowers rattle
in their noisy rest,
the hot color drained
of any recent grief
in such dry display.
Such risky disciplines are the license
the dead may take, they say,
with all false pretenses shed
as we, too, wish, by name, a date's number,
or any other fact so remembered,
to be the final selves we seek
and - like the dowdy angels
made of cheap concrete,
on tip toes, though crumbling -
lean in, a bit off center,
to weather the wearing circles
of the impending sun,
and, looking toward some inner dawn
with our tired interior eyes
when the seething night's advance is done,
we, above our stone-laden stations, rise
and, with a multitude of miracles,
from all disordered dormitories,
anonymous luminaries, moonward fly.

Celestial Mechanics

When man loves stranger
as more than neighbor in his bed,
when twisted heaven falls
and circles of the universe wait
over this changeling of an earth,
the sun revolves within my room
and my eyes hold
a galaxy in place.
Your light reflects
the course from which it came
as our systems prove
affection is stronger
than our loving is strange.

Insect in Amber

Still the acrobat,
the spider spins his filament
across an aeon's space
from that day to this.
His last thin thread trails
past help or hope.
A single twist,
a string of lint,
terminates that tiny rope,
so abrupt, in mute dismay.
There, the brief web he keeps,
broken off in an amber rain,
preserves this painful fact:
disasters have no end;
troubles stop - at death.
That tragedy, though trivial
in this careless world,

77

has earned for its expense
the silences,
though useless,
that monument
an insect's insignificance.
Poised, with no mark of our alarm,
with neither sigh nor rage,
before the cataleptic eye
in the single circus
of his stark and dead
yet death-defying days,
that aerialist hangs
in awesome ways
with those amber arms
and, leaping in the dark
from suspended bar
to a trapeze's sway,
so easy! swings through time,
as any big star does,
on fame from age to age.

Mirrors

When I look in mirrors and am unknown
or see the sun, in perspective, small,
beyond the steep pitch
of this single life's boat
perched on the silver edge
of this tilting earth
at the far end of my eye in eye
and know behind this face I hide,
stranger to myself I am exposed.
Then the sun becomes a judge.
The winds of justice
rise in gales.

But the glaring glass
in which I gaze
is a port as large
as any season's storm would need.
My ship's self-centered eye
waxes, wanes, is lost or found
and I, container of the world I am,
by that other world am contained.
Even in a black rain's heavy night
I transport this broken portion of the sun
which my frail hull's cargo holds
and whose crude journey bears my bones.
Across those dark waters,
calling to the world,
I hear soundings made
to mark the syllables
from word to word
in the calling
of my worldly name.

The Death of the Mite

Even for the mute and unremembered
death of the mite
drowning so early in the dew
of any morning's innocence,
the roar of crowds,
from the world's great chorus of the dead
complains
- like leaves shed, from a hundred storms,
at one sudden season's rush -
and, against the rude
silence of a thousand years,
attests to the rising tide of guilt
that no memorials document

or justify the waste
at the dying end of things
- those sparks, star-like,
that still, willy-nilly, go out.
If no requiems can be sung,
no tolling of the bells,
for the new seed mis-cast,
for the dry-bottomed well,
if only thought's head calls
for the body's time lost
- as an aging athlete sees
in his meticulous mirror
the private note
that the former, public grace,
like any work of art,
is going or is gone -
the disembodied mouth,
though circumspect,
still can sing
some staid and decent song,
and make that dead body dance
in the bodies of the mind.
And if the little theaters of the eyes
remain so tight, so closed,
as if in some dismay,
the silence, though presence still prevails
and moves on in to take its place,
the stillness,
in even the inanimate arrow's cosmic flight,
like the meteor's instant scratch of light,
make the quietude
of the universe
a fitting stone
laid to wait
and mark the place
for multitudes, like those, becalmed,

who lie composed, as if at ease,
and, so, relaxing are contained
or who like us alas, out-cast,
are lost in thought
at that depth of time
and at that distant breadth
extending endless
beyond each earnest mark
of our desperate senses
across such vague
and vast dimensions
as exist
in such tremendous graves.

Shirt Poem

Even your best shirts are frayed.
The seams give out.
Buttons go. At both elbows
the sleeves rip, the body tears
beyond any mending
or hope of any more repair.
The patterns we picked out fade
as flimsy photographs
of a figure's shape
are battered with light,
mottled with age,
flattened out
on their hanging frames.
Their natural force
retreats, involves,
curls in closets like cocoons.
So collars, cuffs, unbuttoned
at the neck and wrist
of a torso's dim silhouette,

almost close around the flesh
but the only bones that are there
are the spare arabesques
bent in the wire
question marks of the hangers.
I buy new clothes these days.
The colors change.
Like the chameleon's tail,
strange arms replace
the wings or the limbs
bullies pull apart.
But the crude stumps
of amputations bud on the bark.
I call them by new names now
- those arms, their embrace.
They are both mine, once again,
as before, but still, we know,
for either arm,
the body is not the same.

The Anatomy Chart

By ancient arrangements the body's innards
in regulation work with all their clocks
like wind-up toys whose gears can't stop
and, wireless, are unattached,
to any source of time or thought
sensing only their torso's body-pain
and never know the worlds gone by
if both the eyes of their busy brain
close down when, spent,
a day-dream's life, dwindling, ends.
As the body-knowledge we extend
depends upon the thought of self
to define its own ideas of identity

and the organs of our sight beyond the mind
explore, like lost microscopes, our outer space
in galaxies to map the charts
to identify each universe we make
that faith or fiction dare create,
what we have at hand, we claim
by touch, hold in name, then, at last,
beyond the Big Bang's start, timeless, let go.
Intelligence celebrates in wonder
the unreal facts we find, verify and date
but which no mind's eye can, really, know
nor our brains' clever waves ever explicate.

Creed

The rock stump of the once-violent volcano,
the calcified trunk from the petrified forest
gorge their thick throat-like shapes with slag
where even the life of the lightning's flash
once had flowed,
or flowers in some stubborn springtime
grew, bloomed, and went to seed.
Even grains of sand record
the clocks of night and day
when each season grinds
the grit of each hard shape
into the polished bits of their identities
needing only names:
so a dead willow's twig,
stuck in mud and water,
offers fat, furry buds
on its barren stick
for green fonts of praise.
Even the articulated post

83

of our own back bones' rod,
set flush within the body's frame,
lets the flesh of our mad hands dance
with some intimate instrument's music
as spontaneous as the ragged ribbons
of a nation's public flags that fly high,
almost frantic, on their May-day shaft.
The rattles of old rituals
shake the cycle of the sun with our belief
and force the fall of some desert's hot rain
or make our Roman candles rise to pierce the dark
as pin-wheels also turn and shed their fire.
We feel the stars shine
through the marrow of our bones.
Their slanting orbits, easy and oblique,
lean in their famous constellations
across the curves of sky
like frozen sparklers of snow
that shower a landscape white.
The sun's erratic course, even so,
is still sure and certain.
Its glitter flows, endless, from its source.
Centered there in a deep dark place,
its pure, bright light
has neither cinders, nor waste.
We praise our moon whose glow
is that same sun we each come from.
At night we count the stars
and deny the terrors of the dark.
To think, to act, to find our name,
we live those kinds of lies we need
to comfort us against the pain of truth
lest our faith in the life of reason
die.

Richard Kostelanetz

(1940 -)

Explores verbal & conceptual nuances through visual representation & the juxtaposition of words or sentences in both random & deliberate sequences, to expand & discover new meanings.

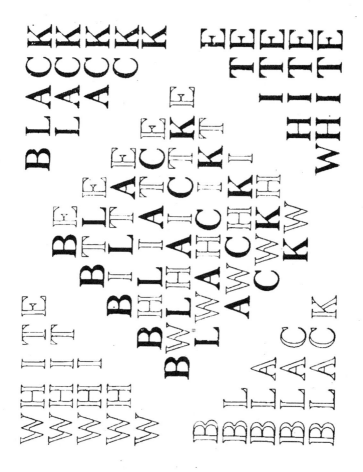

EXHAUSTIVE COMBINATIONS-III

MAN EARTH SPIRIT HEAVEN FAITH
EARTH MAN SPIRIT HEAVEN FAITH
SPIRIT MAN EARTH HEAVEN FAITH
HEAVEN MAN EARTH SPIRIT FAITH
FAITH MAN EARTH SPIRIT HEAVEN
MAN EARTH SPIRIT FAITH HEAVEN
EARTH MAN SPIRIT FAITH HEAVEN
SPIRIT MAN EARTH FAITH HEAVEN
HEAVEN MAN EARTH FAITH SPIRIT
FAITH MAN EARTH HEAVEN SPIRIT
MAN EARTH HEAVEN SPIRIT FAITH
EARTH MAN HEAVEN SPIRIT FAITH
SPIRIT MAN HEAVEN EARTH FAITH
HEAVEN MAN SPIRIT EARTH FAITH
FAITH MAN SPIRIT EARTH HEAVEN
MAN EARTH HEAVEN FAITH SPIRIT
EARTH MAN HEAVEN FAITH SPIRIT
SPIRIT MAN HEAVEN FAITH EARTH
HEAVEN MAN SPIRIT FAITH EARTH
FAITH MAN SPIRIT HEAVEN EARTH
MAN EARTH FAITH SPIRIT HEAVEN
EARTH MAN FAITH SPIRIT HEAVEN
SPIRIT MAN FAITH EARTH HEAVEN
HEAVEN MAN FAITH EARTH SPIRIT
FAITH MAN HEAVEN EARTH SPIRIT
MAN EARTH FAITH HEAVEN SPIRIT
EARTH MAN FAITH HEAVEN SPIRIT
SPIRIT MAN FAITH HEAVEN EARTH
HEAVEN MAN FAITH SPIRIT EARTH
FAITH MAN HEAVEN SPIRIT EARTH
MAN SPIRIT EARTH HEAVEN FAITH
EARTH SPIRIT MAN HEAVEN FAITH
SPIRIT EARTH MAN HEAVEN FAITH

HEAVEN EARTH MAN SPIRIT FAITH
FAITH EARTH MAN SPIRIT HEAVEN
MAN SPIRIT EARTH FAITH HEAVEN
EARTH SPIRIT MAN FAITH HEAVEN
SPIRIT EARTH MAN FAITH HEAVEN
HEAVEN EARTH MAN FAITH SPIRIT
FAITH EARTH MAN HEAVEN SPIRIT
MAN SPIRIT HEAVEN EARTH FAITH
EARTH SPIRIT HEAVEN MAN FAITH
SPIRIT EARTH HEAVEN MAN FAITH
HEAVEN EARTH SPIRIT MAN FAITH
FAITH EARTH SPIRIT MAN HEAVEN
MAN SPIRIT HEAVEN FAITH EARTH
EARTH SPIRIT HEAVEN FAITH MAN
SPIRIT EARTH HEAVEN FAITH MAN
HEAVEN EARTH SPIRIT FAITH MAN
FAITH EARTH SPIRIT HEAVEN MAN
MAN SPIRIT FAITH EARTH HEAVEN
EARTH SPIRIT FAITH MAN HEAVEN
SPIRIT EARTH FAITH MAN HEAVEN
HEAVEN EARTH FAITH MAN SPIRIT
FAITH EARTH HEAVEN MAN SPIRIT
MAN SPIRIT FAITH HEAVEN EARTH
EARTH SPIRIT FAITH HEAVEN MAN
SPIRIT EARTH FAITH HEAVEN MAN
HEAVEN EARTH FAITH SPIRIT MAN
FAITH EARTH HEAVEN SPIRIT MAN
MAN HEAVEN EARTH SPIRIT FAITH
EARTH HEAVEN MAN SPIRIT FAITH
SPIRIT HEAVEN MAN EARTH FAITH
HEAVEN SPIRIT MAN EARTH FAITH
FAITH SPIRIT MAN EARTH HEAVEN
MAN HEAVEN EARTH FAITH SPIRIT
EARTH HEAVEN MAN FAITH SPIRIT
SPIRIT HEAVEN MAN FAITH EARTH
HEAVEN SPIRIT MAN FAITH EARTH
FAITH SPIRIT MAN HEAVEN EARTH

MAN HEAVEN SPIRIT EARTH FAITH
EARTH HEAVEN SPIRIT MAN FAITH
SPIRIT HEAVEN EARTH MAN FAITH
HEAVEN SPIRIT EARTH MAN FAITH
FAITH SPIRIT EARTH MAN HEAVEN
MAN HEAVEN SPIRIT FAITH EARTH
EARTH HEAVEN SPIRIT FAITH MAN
SPIRIT HEAVEN EARTH FAITH MAN
HEAVEN SPIRIT EARTH FAITH MAN
FAITH SPIRIT HEAVEN MAN EARTH
MAN HEAVEN FAITH SPIRIT EARTH
EARTH HEAVEN FAITH SPIRIT MAN
SPIRIT HEAVEN FAITH EARTH MAN
HEAVEN SPIRIT FAITH EARTH MAN
FAITH SPIRIT HEAVEN EARTH MAN
MAN FAITH EARTH SPIRIT HEAVEN
EARTH FAITH MAN SPIRIT HEAVEN
SPIRIT FAITH MAN EARTH HEAVEN
HEAVEN FAITH MAN EARTH SPIRIT
FAITH HEAVEN MAN EARTH SPIRIT
MAN FAITH EARTH HEAVEN SPIRIT
EARTH FAITH MAN HEAVEN SPIRIT
SPIRIT FAITH MAN HEAVEN EARTH
HEAVEN FAITH MAN SPIRIT EARTH
FAITH HEAVEN MAN SPIRIT EARTH
MAN FAITH SPIRIT EARTH HEAVEN
EARTH FAITH SPIRIT MAN HEAVEN
SPIRIT FAITH EARTH MAN HEAVEN
HEAVEN FAITH EARTH MAN SPIRIT
FAITH HEAVEN EARTH MAN SPIRIT
MAN FAITH SPIRIT HEAVEN EARTH
EARTH FAITH SPIRIT HEAVEN MAN
SPIRIT FAITH EARTH HEAVEN MAN
HEAVEN FAITH EARTH SPIRIT MAN
FAITH HEAVEN EARTH SPIRIT MAN
MAN FAITH HEAVEN EARTH SPIRIT
EARTH FAITH HEAVEN MAN SPIRIT

```
SPIRIT FAITH HEAVEN MAN EARTH
HEAVEN FAITH SPIRIT MAN EARTH
FAITH HEAVEN SPIRIT MAN EARTH
MAN FAITH HEAVEN SPIRIT EARTH
EARTH FAITH HEAVEN SPIRIT MAN
SPIRIT FAITH HEAVEN EARTH MAN
HEAVEN FAITH SPIRIT EARTH MAN
FAITH HEAVEN SPIRIT EARTH MAN
```

```
R                        P
RE                      I P
REL                    H I P
RELA                 SH I P
RELAT            N SH I P
RELATIONSH I P
RELATIONSH I P
RELAT            N SH I P
RELA                 SH I P
REL                    H I P
RE                      I P
R                        P
```

MULTIPLE GHOSTS

ACKNOWLEDGE
ACTIVATE
ACTION
ADDITION
ADDRESSING
ADVANTAGE
ADVICE
AIRPLANE
ALLEVIATE
ALONGSIDE
ALTERNATE
AMBIDEXTROUS
AMBIGUOUS
ANCHOR
ANNOUNCE
ANTICIPATE
ANYMORE
APPROACH
APPOINT
ASPHALT
ASSEMBLED
ASTONISHING
ATTRACTION
ATTACKING
AUTOBIOGRAPHY
AUTHORITIES
BARRAGE
BASSOON
BEATEN
BEAUTIFY
BECOME
BEHOLD
BELIEVER
BENEFIT

BIOGRAPHY
BLOW
BOTHERED
BRILLIANT
BUSINESSMAN
CARRIAGE
COITION
CONTINUOUS
CORPORATION
CRYSTALLINE
DEMONSTRATES
DIFFERENT
DIGNITIES
DIRECTOR
DISADVANTAGE
DISCONTENTS
DISHONEST
DOCTOR
DOLLARBILL
ECHOES
EMANCIPATE
ENORMOUS
EVERYTHING
EVERYWHERE
FASHION
FINISHED
FAMILIAR
FEATURING
FOREFATHER
FORESTRY
FUNDAMENTAL
FUNEREAL
GENERALLY
GOVERNMENT
GUNFIRE
HANDWRITTEN

HEARING
HIDEOUS
HISTAMINE
HISTORIAN
HORIZON
HORSEMEN
ILLITERACY
IMMEDIATE
IMMIGRATION
IMPACT
IMPLICIT
INDIVIDUALITY
INEQUALITY
INHIBITED
INORDINATE
INSEPARABLE
INTEREST
INTRODUCE
INTRODUCTION
KNOWLEDGE
LANDLORD
LANDMARK
LANGUAGE
LITTLEST
LOWERING
MAJORITIES
MANDATE
MANUFACTURING
MARKETPLACE
MARRIAGE
MEASURE
MEDITATE
MEETING
MELODIES
MELODIOUS
MEMORY

MENTION
MERCIFULLY
METAMORPHOSIS
METROPOLIS
MILLION
MINORITIES
MONUMENT
MUSICOLOGIST
NEIGHBOR
NEWSPAPER
NOMINATE
NORTHERN
NOTORIOUS
NOURISHMENT
NUMBERED
ORGANIZATION
ORIGIN
OURSELVES
OWNERSHIP
PARTICULATE
PASSION
PASTIME
PENCHANT
PENTECOST
PHARMACIST
PHONOGRAPH
PHOTOGRAPHER
PLAYWRIGHT
PRINCIPAL
PUBLISHER
ORCHARD
RAMPART
REALITIES
RESTAURANT
REPRESENTATIVE
SHEPHERD

SINGLED
SITUATE
SITUATION
SKYSCRAPER
SOCIOLOGICAL
SOMEWHERE
SOVEREIGN
SPLENDOR
SUBSCRIBE
TEACHER
TENACITY
THEMSELVES
THOUSAND
TOLERANT
TOMORROW
TORTURED
TRANSPOSE
TURNTABLE
UNSOPHISTICATED
UPBRAID
UPDATE
USUALLY
VANISHED
VARIATIONS
WANDERED
WEARING
WELCOME
WELFARE
WHEELCHAIR
WINDMILL
WINTERTIME
YESTERDAY
YOUNGEST

WALK THE EARTH
RESUSCITATE
INVIGORATE
PROPAGATE
ENERGIZE
ACTIVATE
CONTINUE
TURN ON
BREATHE
ANIMATE
SUBSIST
PREVAIL
ENDURE
THRIVE
VIVIFY
ROUSE
ABIDE
EXIST
LIVE

ELEVEN EAGER ETHEREAL EAGLES EVADE ETERNITY EASILY EVIL EGOISM ETIOLOGY EVAPORATE EVENTUALLY ELECTIVE ELECTRIC ECHO ESCHEW EGREGIOUS ELEPHANTIASIS ELUCIDATE EMOLUMENT EVALUATION EQUANIMITY INVINCIBLE ERADICATE ELECTRIC ECONOMY EVISCERATE EBULLIENT EASEL EGRESS EGALITARIAN EMASCULATE ERECTION ERUPT EQUIVOCATE EQUESTRIAN EQUIPS EVANGELIST ENUMERATE ESOPHAGUS EQUIVALENT EDITION ELIMINATE ENIGMA EQUATION ETIOLOGY ELITE EMOTION EQUALIZE ENOUGH

98

from 1001 Opera Libretti
for John F. Cone

A young couple, universally attractive and recently married, attempt to defy a new state law forbidding procreation, their arias proclaiming erotic success, in spite of the relentless maneuverings of their anxious parents and mean police.

A terminally ill insurance investigator initiates a complicated scheme to be charged with murder and thus sentenced to death, prompting his family to collect a generous insurance settlement; but for reasons beyond his control, his plans go posthumously awry.

Just after a young girl learns the facts of life from a beloved aunt who is dying, love blossoms, prompting the girl to break away from the mother surrogate to become an independent adult.

A masked rider becomes a hero for the oppressed, successfully stealing from the rich to give to the poor until a conflagration caused by Nature causes his untimely death.

A diva falls deeply in love with the hidden prompter to the disappointment of the highly visible conductor.

The butler and housekeeper pretend to be masters of the house when their boss is away.

The young woman who inherits the factory that employs most of a small town falls in love with a laborer whom her relatives forbid her to marry, to the audible distress of everyone else in her neighborhood.

Two couples, assigned to share the same apartment during a housing shortage, find themselves falling in love with one another in unexpected, calamitous ways, the quality of their arias changing during the performance from mellow at the beginning to antagonistic at the end.

A young immigrant, joining a local street gang, makes the tactical mistake of becoming the secret lover of the gang leader's freshly nubile daughter in an autobiographical opera left unfinished by the composer's untimely death.

The prince and the princess are a dull married couple until the prince takes a mistress and the princess disguises herself as a singing streetwalker in order to win him back. .

The quality of a woman's voice changes, along with her love life, after she undergoes extensive plastic surgery.

Three traveling salesmen, friends as well as competitors, flirt with love objects of different ages and different sorts during their visit to a small city.

A young man with over-protective parents is invited to the beach and then initiated into adulthood by his mother's best friend.

A predatory general is brought to trial at the entrance to heaven and, before a tribunal of common people, is sentenced to death for his crimes against humanity, notwithstanding his claim to have served his country in over one hundred battles.

Housewives go to a bar, open only during daylight hours, where they can live out their romantic fantasies with otherwise unemployed men.

A newly famous, freshly wealthy writer moves his family to the suburbs where his wife falls in love with his publisher.

A young man, caught between two desirous women, is ultimately uninterested in either.

An intricate, morally ambiguous drama about life at the top of a multinational corporation on the verge of bankruptcy disintegrates into a familiarly simple romance between the president and, no joke, his "vice-president for corporate affairs."

A series of flashbacks reveals that a theatrical agent has, as a spurned suitor, killed the prima donna he has promoted to professional success.

A high-flying fashion designer falls in love with a retired athlete, who brings her down to earth, initially in a billiards parlor.

While investigating a murder, the chief of police inadvertently kills a woman whose death he conceals while continuing the initial search.

A widow marries a widower, who very much in love with each other, want to move all their children into the same modest apartment house.

A long-standing feud between two families blows up when the daughter of one elopes with, and then is impregnated by, the son of another.

Marrying on the rebound a man who actually abuses her, she works up enough disgust, and courage, to shoot her husband as a rapist.

A widower marrying his late wife's sister frequently addresses her with the dead woman's name.

The sheriff who accidentally kills a policeman is legally obliged to care for his colleague's widow and several children.

All the girl friends to whom the traveling salesman has given his apartment key suddenly, and unexpectedly, show up at his home.

Two clowns disguise themselves as police detectives when the circus ringmaster is murdered, fooling not only real policemen but the killer.

An old-maid college professor, at a professional convention, invites several male colleagues to her hotel room, and later charges them with rape, though each insists under oath that he was voluntarily seduced.

In a pocket of a jacket left to her for repairs a lonely woman tailor finds a love letter that gives her so much vicarious pleasure that she neglects the electric pressing equipment, accidentally setting off a fire alarm; but among her rescuers is a handsome fireman who, before returning to work, makes a date for the following Saturday night.

An attractive young woman sleeps with enough enemy soldiers to penetrate the headquarters, where she swiftly decapitates the general of the army besieging her city.

The dictator who rapes his virgin sister-in-law, cutting out her tongue to prevent her from reporting the crime to his wife, in turn suffers revenge when the mute woman kills his eldest male child, her nephew, and serves the boy's roasted body at a royal feast.

A politically awakened wife of a corporate mogul marries her husband's anarchist executioner.

After a couple moves from one city to another, the husband discovers, in the course of making love to his wife, that she has become a human radio receiver, thanks to the silver fillings in her teeth.

An aging opera singer, unable to accept declining powers, spends most of her spare time continually seducing ever younger starlets.

Two girls meet three soldiers, who vie with one another for each girl's favors until they all decide it would be better for all if they were joined by a third girl.

A newspaper reporter whose specialty is exposing political corruption makes everyone suspicious by marrying the widow of a slain gangster.

When a group of male travelers become stranded on a sandbar at high tide, one of them robs and murders a banker, absconding as well with his mistress.

The princess who mysteriously loses her breasts becomes a man, prompting her outraged husband, the prince, to become a woman if the illusion of royal normalcy is to be preserved, causing so much confusion, both private and public, that both decide simultaneously to resume their original sexual identities.

A young woman is determined to find the people responsible for the unsolved crime in which her father lost his life.

A happily married contemporary couple get into a marriage-shattering fight after viewing a film about life on a primitive island.

A repellingly ugly beggar inexplicably attracts a series of stunningly attractive women.

A married woman teases her former rival-in-love about her inability to find a husband, while the audience recognizes that the single woman actually has the more fortunate life.

The wife of a dead gangster reluctantly marries his slayer who is tormented by memories of his yet undetected crime and is induced to confess when he suspects, several months later, that his ex-wife's child might have actually been fathered by her previous husband.

A teenager plants a bomb that blows up the personal car used by the chief of the invaders who had desecrated sacred lands and murdered his mother and sister.

The father of our country not only brings warring factions together but he invents love.

A reluctant bridegroom jumps out of a ground-floor window in order to escape marriage and, he thinks, swift divorce.

After two political dissidents are beheaded, their widows, on hand to claim their husbands' bodies, argue passionately over which torso belongs to which head.

A chorus girl, in love with the theater's assistant manager, gently resists the amorous advances of an electrician whom she also knows as the assistant manager's best friend.

Nurses who organize to expose doctors' duplicitous dealings in illicit drugs eat hospital food that, to their surprise, makes them deathly ill.

A young man, spurned by his girl friend, retires to a monastery only to discover that, because of insufficient piety, he must return to a sensual reunion with his apologetic lover.

A blind woman, witnessing a murder, tries to convince the police, as well as the audience, of the truth of her testimony.

When a man accidentally encounters the greatest love of his life, whom he mistakenly rejected twenty years before, each is them is prompted to remember the affair and their lives since.

A young wife is trying to locate her missing husband, who has accidentally witnessed a gangland murder, before the assassins do.

Though a nightmare-ridden woman discovers that the killers in her dreams actually roam the streets of her neighborhood, her policeman husband doesn't believe her.

A fraudulent psychic cons himself into experiencing hallucinations and in terror murders his crippled assistant, believing him to be haunted.

L

L
L
Y
P
O
P

Lyn
Lifshin
(1944 -   )

*Reveals psychological truths using emotional snapshots
within the context of a massive body of work that is
in continuous maturation. Her perceptions are
intuitive but detailed, expressing the poet's
complex view of herself & the world.*

That February

Snow on your hair,
the room so warm and
everything melting,
there we thought of
starting but it was all
over, that's the way
it had to stay. Dust
in our throats, the same
dried flowers on the wall
and we leaving half relieved
clutching iced branches,
glad for the cold

Chihuahua Coahuila

drove for days in
the rose and blue
light of the desert
stoned on names
ocotillo, coral beans
by the sixth day the
aloneness got us   there
wasn't a face or voice
not even near the
hogans   nights   we slept
in the car with the
doors locked   locked
in ourselves we were
like skin peeled from a
finger, shriveling
having nothing to do
with any hand

109

Please Let Me Be

Please let me be

your lady
    this torn
house   the
weeds   love we

could just
watch the
    ·   lake

in one corner

listen to
leaves to
    what the

shutters say
nights

In Vermont

In Vermont in
rooms plain grey and
wooden
I remember his sitting
those nights without
a word and
how he stood in the park,
listening to chestnuts dropping,
but not much else.

Please Send a Short Note

as you know the
houses i live
in dissolve are
like snow legs
in a blizzard
less real than
the houses i
sat around in
stoned on the
lives of other
women   i'm most
comfortable with
ruins   rings the
bones in back
of glass   after
i write poems
i learn to do
what happens in
them and know
as soon as i
don't want some
thing i can
have it

It Came Screaming Thru the Branches

It came screaming
thru the branches
leaving the plane
a swayback bird
sunk in the torn

house all
night cutting
the dead and
moaning out
snow falling
now these
oranges in the
bloody snow
gasoline strips
of polaroid
people park
cars walk
up the roped
streets with
cameras stand
in front of the
twisted tail
holding their
children tight

Lips

lips   fingers on my
back pulling wanting
to get down what can't
stay like Monet trapping
magical colors what
transformed noon
something in me is the
cat tunneling in under
the quilt over the
electric blanket making
a warm sandwich as
wind blows maples bare

Mulberry Madonna

Mulberry Madonna
goes out early
even before any
pheasants her
feet are purple

then later while
it's still light
she puts a blanket
under the mulberry

shaking the branches
huge pails of
mulberries purple
wool purple
fingers and
that mulberry kiss

Low Tide

low tide

tiny black snails moving
over the flats

fish in the tide pools

mint on her skin   the
seeds carried
from leydon

sand burns
under a nail

grain shifting
pollen on the water

the sun   her belly
straining against the
cloth that keeps getting tighter

Gulls In The Blue Air

gulls in the blue air
a woman watching

frozen salmon sun
the bristles of
stiff pine   she

leans close

linseed smell like
someplace in england
bayberries like pewter

their sweet smoke
in her hair   the
night a necklace

of birds
snow   if she
could just write
someone this

Madonna With a Broken Gun

a broken cat
the 22 under
a pillow

madonna with
broken zippers
from rushing too
fast into
or away

broken house
broken window

madonna with
a gun under

feeling the piece
of roof falling

a gun in
side some

wanting but
not sure if
she can put
much together

The Houses So Small

The houses so small
baskets like Indian women
to carry and store
things in

baskets of thimbles
yarn and needles

boxes carved with
grapes and bees

smokey rooms
with so little room

the dresses had to have
huge pockets   there

were so few places
to stretch out

Shrinking Madonna

her skin is so
delicate you can
almost see the
nerve endings
capillaries
break down dont
dream its just
no vitamin c or
that she's pull
ing into her

self like some
leaf growing
backward its the
incredible shrink
ing its some
thing growing turn
ing to stone the
dirt on that
leaf pressed in
to fossil pressed
hard and thin
leaves in a book
nobody opens
she's so thin
when she shaves
her arm pits the
hair's too deep
in to reach
like her anger

Embroidered Wedding Picture

Embroidered Wedding Picture
from some
where in New England
Hannah Green
stitching this with
green silk on
linen while a north
wind blew the cherry trees
blew white leaves
on the store walk
looked like snow in april
she felt the needle
scratch her hand

117

cat howling near
the stove   she stops   starts
again   the rose is done   1756   the
bride is small   dissolves
between the two men
stitched in bright
colors in the
foreground

Painting of Elizabeth and Mary Daggert

one holding a doll
the other is poking
her finger in its
eyes   the children
dressed like the
doll all in white
the one with the
finger in the eye
smirks as if
she knows she'll be
trapped in a life
like a doll's where
you couldn't do
this to a baby
so she does it now

Another Wedding Picture

most of the women have
little faces   often no
lips   no eyes   as if

not to see the men
in the foreground   laughing

the horse is more de
tailed than any women are

huge red bird
bigger than anything
floats at the top
of the page
way over the church

all the windows
barred like a prison

blue sky with big
bugs flying in it

the wedding on coach

black like a little
cave or cell

Mourning Pictures

in silk and water color
9 people in black
with enormous hankies
lying against the
tomb that's draped
with flowers   in back
the weeping willow
trees   lean like a
woman with her hair
loose, flowing

Women In Front Of A High Case Of Mirrors, Bureau Mirrors, Hall Mirrors, Mirrors In Frames Of Wood, Gold, Tin Silver

When she sees so
many reflections,
too many to focus on
she thinks of her
garden, how it
might have
worked if he had
helped her cut
away what went
so wild, too tangled
to see a way thru, like
so much between
them. The roots
needed what they
didn't get. When she
sees her eyes
lowered in the
glass she steps back.
It's too much to
deal with, tho it
might be easier in
the dark, where she
can't see that it's
taken this long to
see how what hasn't
been shaped and cared
for now can just be
hacked away

Inland Maine

jasmine tea,
iced apples

hair fell across
my face drifting
upstairs
in a sweet
smoke, cherry
burning, this
paper smells
of those
fires i
want to too.

Dinner Plate

dinner plate of
hand painted blue
and white porcelain

violet embroidered
birds on an apron
that doesn't look
like it was used

blood, green and amber
beads threaded
on a small bag

most women who wanted
to do something
painted things in
the house

or kept a diary
some diary in
their blood no one
read signed me, me

Rachelle Weeping   Painting 1772

some mothers   lived to
bury all their children

charles peale   his baby
dying of small pox
painted the child
quiet as stone
her arms tied with
a satin ribbon
at her side

lace covered pillow
the sheets over the
bottom of her legs
like a little orange
on a pillow

years later he painted
the mother in tears
touching her ownskin

resting at the
edge of the bed
like it was a
table she was studying her home
work on

the picture hung years
in the painter's house
covered by a curtain

with the sign "Before you
draw this curtain consider
whether you will
offend a mother or father
who has lost a child"

Hannka lamp

Hannka lamp
of tin and iron

11 inches
circa 1790

in Ipswich
December   the cranberries
frozen   little
shriveled rubies

night smells of
beachplum   pine

the lights flicker on
the hair and plaster ceiling

turns pewter   rose
some father holding
his daughter   closer

prays this country
will want them
more than the last

Thinking of What a

Thinking of what a
woman could be

blue bed, the
bluest blues

There's so little
not to share

Dream Of Ivy

You know the story of
the woman in a
turret and how ivy
puts its fingers
across the moon.
And besides, no one
could hear. Ivy
that grows like
kudzu in the
deepest part of Georgia
swallowing up a
single house
in one night. I would
have lowered my long
hair to a lover
lured him with blood
in a bottle, each
drop a ruby with
a poem etched on it
or carved my initials
in the grey stone
around his heart. I'd

have talked to the
birds or waited
slept 20 years given
away my children.
Only I was outside
trying to get in.

Vanity, Thy Name Is Woman

over the round
mirror like the
two in my mother's
dark rooms Otter
Falls rushed and
blurred the sounds
of fights in.
Hand mirrors
dangle, bacalite
and silver, gold,
as if to spit
back so much
the one standing in
front of them,
as if they were
judge and jury, is
dazzled, damaged.
Smaller mirrors
taunt, reflections
of reflections and
I think of standing
in front of my
mother's vanity,
raising my skirt
in terror to
check thighs

I never thought
wouldn't be
flabby and fat
tho in certain
rose light,
the edges softened.
After I left
and then came
back home, after
stepping tentatively
on the bathroom scale
when my mother was
shopping, I'd
make it thru her
clutter, over
the Johnson's Baby
powder, to inspect
and examine, hunt
for flaws. It
was more brutal to pick
up one of her hand
mirrors and
catch a look
at what someone would
see from behind, tho my
mother always said strangers
stopped her on the
street, said what
a beauty. The backs
of the mirrors with
inlay, or plastic
roses, wouldn't have
scorched, but like
someone who can't
not slow down, crane
their neck at an
accident, I move

closer, as I did
in those rooms I thought
the mirror would
never not be in, as a
touchstone, to chastise
and scold, like
a mother who glues
her daughter to her
outlining her short
comings as if by
making her need to
get her approval,
she'll keep her
hooked

Now When I Don't Want You Blues

you catch a whiff
of rose and our knees crumble

I'd like to say it took one night for
you to call but it's been years

You did the work, making me
up as you wanted. Then, you said

I whined. I drank too much.
You've even got the color

of my dress wrong: I never
wear orange. But if it pleases you,

I'll play along like any woman
faking orgasm. You think my

cheetah thighs, yours then,
were the silkiest, my mouth a

national treasure. There was
danger you write, my high heels

so close to your face.
So what if I was in ballet

shoes or sandals. I'll
go along, knowing

the farther I get from you
in time the more

you want me

Lilly Of The Valley

cologne, I would give
it to you, your favorite
flower after lilacs.
I planted the white
bells, dug them up for
my back yard, took
some pale pink ones
too. The cologne,
somehow too sweet,
maybe there's
jasmin in it. It's so
long since I used your
Joy up. I could have
left the *Muget de Bois*,
I'll check to see if
this lily of the valley
is in the trees on

your grave. With all
the shade from the
maple you thought
would be peaceful,
moss is covering the
granite. A psychic on
Larry King said if you
talk to the dead they
hear, will give you
a sign, knock on the
window, a stillness on
the phone. I wish I
believed her, remember
how we talked of
putting a phone in your
casket, how, queen
of phone calls and
tracking people down
thru AT & T, we bet
that if anyone could get
thru it would be you

Cat Love

pillow or worn cotton
Shirt it would be ok
about loving it. But
cat love is a risky
choice. It sounds so
sentimental and this
isn't even a dead or
dying cat. Lets say it
is not a cat but say
an old bathrobe you
feel comfortable in

as a broken in lover
where it's ok to be
quiet, not charming.
Lets call my cat a
bathrobe and think
of curling deep in
soft chenille - make
it rose for the hint
this cold March day
of new buds unfolding.
Think of her as some
thing to wear, which
I do. Haven't you
made a blanket of
your dog or cat, let
him lie on you like a
lover, felt its heart and
breath moving with
your breath, so close
to the parts of you
that you share with
your lover that when
you sleep her soft fur
could be his fingers?

Harry
Smith
(1936 -   )

*Uses the projective form to convey patterns of
consciousness, & melds metrical poetry with prose
to objectify experience in a stylistic synthesis.
He believes that poets have the primary
responsibility for the description of history.*

Me, the People

Me the people had enough.   Out of the gorge of city
this glittering Bicentennial I come,
fat & discontent   after my feasty Christmastide,
down to dark, stilled docks trimmed with Yule electric glit
at grayday unseen sundown   and watch the steel
dusk deepening across my home harbor
                        most fabulous and most dreamed -

My Lady of Liberty,
                        Seen everywhere, beckoning...
            Thy sister isle of immigrants lies
lightless, closed.   I see it dimly, image
fading into night   relic towers
ghostly   blackbourne   derelict
            the corpse of a dream
Ellis Island, last stop before the shores of dream.

        My Yiddishers named it The Isle of Tears.
That crowded, redbrick Immigration Works processed
Esteke
    of Warsaw, removing her with her five small children
    from the moving line when the medical inspector found
    trachoma in her unforgotten eyes   never to see
    her husband in New York.
Tears. I speak those tears   at the far end of hope,

        each coming ship leaving a story to give the name
once more:
INZL FOON TRERN
        I weep. This Bicentennial Christmas of our graven
past,

I weep for my Yids. All my brave, bewildered
greenhorns, I see them
    my amazed millions, herded through mazed,
sweating corridors,
  and waiting in the echoing great hall (like a Balkan
    ministry's):
  dapper adventurers and proud peasants in their
    vari-spendid
       native garbs, or the tidied tatters of the disposed:
      Benita,
         the five-year old Palermo girl holding her first
    penny like a star
-O shiny New! -
Spring tides of history tossing on America!
A twenty-seven acre isle, dump for ships' ballast, Army
ammo dump,
    made the main pumping station for the overflow of
nations
                            into the open continent

New World,
I see the terrific progeny on the expressway
Herding: here, hard by the overhead HUZZ of traffic, the
unnatural
    haze of wastes (farts to kill the world!)
I see the destined city dimming this year in a time of
shortages,
    energy ebbing,   new slab skyscrapers cemeterial,
the capital of the world, of mightiest manworks, failing.
I inhale the stench of the elderly poor, uncollected garbage
    and abandoned tenements, and the sick air corroding
    the souvenir bronze of Liberty
                  Liberty Enlightening the World?
I mutter, disconsolate.   The winter of our Bicentennial.
my coldest winter. The energy crisis. The future starved?
The bloat of Europe's hopes?

I behold the litter of the plastic generation and the idiot
grins,
    Of incessant autos brighteyed, lifelike in their bilateral
symmetry.
The Promised Destiny I mourn. I falter, my own energy
    draining... No! I rage primeval! My being moves
outward
across waters like a ferry's slow, strong
gliding progress to The Isle of Tears,
European-looking buildings, empty, spiritless.

I unthing the place!   -They vanish.   I put all in its earlier
order
    - before Sam Ellis got begat,
   before any Dutchman told of Oyster Island -
the way it was, say, when the Carnarsee raced down to The
Narrows
    to see Giovanni Verrazano's outlandish vessel
    passing through dreamlike to Minnissais
                         Great Oyster Bay

I magick the vision. I make it a future. (I am absolute!)
   my beautiful potentialities, Me, dreamer & dreamt,
the tuned mote resonant with the world!
The sacred anger of the prophet rests.
I am where the dream went,
    carrier, vehicle, Me, remerging with my traffic,
    gray noise & the unharmonious special decibels,
registering
    the modern composition, our dominant transit, Me
transistor.
Me continuum.

from Trinity 9/11

Day 26
October 6
Back. Rector & Greenwich.
Why this corner?
Hamilton watched the work, as the cranes waved American
flags in the smoke
      Dust
Toxic particles?   dioxins asbestos lead mercury
                Wear the mask that Margaret gave me?
He donned the white biohazard mask. Please her.
Hamilton looked above the sharp shards and twisted
wreckage to the pale blue-gray haze and saw a city in the sky.
Rising from Ground Zero, it was not his plan but science
fiction coming true, towers far taller than the fallen twins.
Linked by skyways with pedestrian conveyor belts, topped by
parks and ornamented by elegant terraces, awesome edifices
of stainless steel and silver-tinted glass shone in the sunlight.

Hamilton looked down at the feet. He trembled at a
sudden darkening of the day
The shadow of the future
Just a cloud crossing the sun.

He looked at the crowd. Come to bear witness always so
many.
Like Carol: He noticed a woman who reminded him of his
daughter
40ish bony blonde But sexy. Carol's anything but sexy.
Deliberately dowdy. This young woman was wearing a faded
blue denim skirt zippered on the side, showing a
black-stocking leg up to mid-thigh. Odd, Here, so many
women in sexy outfits. He thought of Carol. Determinedly
plain. Dressed like the school girls she teaches. Why is she so

136

so   Androgynous?
                   Virgin?
No sign of female lovers
                        Discreet?
Androgyny
a
sex a
sexual
Internet Sperm
"Oh, John, she threatens to have artificial insemination."
Margaret. Almost wailing.
Seminate
The Hamilton line
His
Hamilton wanted to be a grandfather.
The succession
My own success
Succeeding
Myself
Fault? My fault?
                   Too strict? Too cold?
                   To Margaret? To Carol?
                   Too   petty?
Small
Hamilton saw himself as small.
Don't they know, damn it? I love
A small family   Not happy enough?
"Be realistic, Margaret. I'll gladly settle for an internet
grandchild."
"I haven't reproached her, John."
                        By your silence, Margaret
"You don't mind, Daddy?" Almost incredulous.
"No, I don't mind, Dear."
He remembered Carol kissing his cheek.
"That's the nicest thing you ever said to me, Daddy."
He winced inwardly. The nicest? He felt ashamed.
Damned WASP

Typical WASP? My own cold upbringing
Poor Carol
          Wasps
People like ants bees termites wasps
Swarming
Once more he saw the hiving future.

Of sperm, I sing, and future swarms and the chill shadow of
the city of the future on us.
Day What?   Lost count in Rome.

October 24, 2001
Day 44
THE DOORS OF TRINITY CHURCH
WILL SOON OPEN WIDE
ONCE MORE
Reassuring sign
He entered it in his journal, noting
strong Roman type, white on green; black border; white
margins.
In the churchyard
                    tiny florescent orange flags   markers?
                              points of blast damage?
Thus removal of a headstone?
His next entry:
Broadway & Cedar
        W: yellow crane against damaged NE façade of
        Battery Park City
140 Cedar: once home of City Midday Club (defunct).
Bldg closed. Blown out windows high on Bwy side
facing WTC
        The red Noguchi sculpture like a giant nut
        balanced threateningly on a point where two sides
join.

138

Hamilton coughed. He wrote
The smoldering   the acrid smell   like what? —burning
plastic. PCBs. Dioxins.
Some passersby in white bio masks. When will it stop
burning?
Smoldering embers
He recalled an old song
            Love's smoldering embers
Here are
        Hate's smoldering embers

Love? the future of love the fate of love The Triumph of
Love?
Heartsick. No need to write it down. A man felt heartsick.
Low, slow, small, seen through the gap on Liberty Street, a
plane flew over The Pile. A helicopter flew downtown along
Broadway.

LIBERTY PLAZA

ironic or prophetic?
Open again
Long table in the lobby: Security Checks: Everyone had
photo IDs.
Hamilton had his new photo ID for tenants. No reason to go
in. The building was open, but his office was still closed. Its
regular operation would resume soon, but his routines
seemed meaningless.
The odd blackness.
He had become inured to the peculiar aspect of his
building but saw it fresh, the slabs of polished black granite
around it, black-tinted reflecting windows, steel columns
painted dull black:
Funereal
"The Darth Vader Building"

139

—words of his neighbor Cathy, as if she were
speaking in his ear.
Assyrian: Hamilton regarded the large, gleaming stone
marker for One Liberty Plaza, whereon the names of the
principal tenants were inscribed. Assyrian stele We haven't
changed
A big jet plane flew over the WTC site
        Liner?
        Bomber?
        Liner
His nose and throat burned. The smoke seemed as bad as in
the early days after the attack. Two old ladies in business
suits talked of anthrax.
He looked at the NASDAQ logo, gray on black, on their
side of the main entrance, before deciding to walk north to
St. Paul's Chapel.

He stopped at the next corner to take out his notebook:
Bwy & Maiden Ln: best view of smoke, belching like a
volcano, despite ceaseless great arc of water pouring down on
it, cooling the jaws of back hoes
A leaflet was thrust in front of his face. He took it.
No weapon formed
against you shall prosper
Where from?
Christian proselytizers everywhere
Onward
        Uptown

The IT behind
The NYSE
Powering 7 out of 10 trades
On Wall Street
Sybase information anywhere

The man marveled at the outdoor sign, yellow type on a
girder-red field. Absurdly impressive.
The infortun of marte. Ah, Chaucer.
At Broadway & Dey, he gazed across the ruins to What?
Wheels?

                    Like concentric Ferris wheels
Pointing, he asked a young policeman, "What am I
seeing?"
"The Atrium. The Winter Garden. Between the World
Financial Center Buildings. Remarkable it stood up. It had
great views of the river."
"Maybe they should leave it as a monument."
"They don't know what to do. Maybe rebuild the whole
thing." The policeman shrugged and smiled. Hamilton
liked him.
"Yes, they will build a new World Trade Center. I just hope
they'll leave something in remembrance."
"They probably will."

Hamilton nodded, smiled, walked several feet away and
stopped to make another note:
Perhaps the relic Atrium should be part of the memorial
park.
Odd: Oblivious   He wondered why he had been oblivious to
it before.
Oblivious: As he walked toward St. Paul's, he realized he
had developed the habit of not looking at the pleas for the
missing, the messages to the dead and the improvised
shrines and memorials posted along Broadway in line
Ground Zero. Pathetic.   All dead.

Rickshaws.
He watched a bicycle taxi, a strong young man
transporting a middle-aged man in an elegant dark suit.
Something new. Practical.

Standing in front of St. Paul's, still closed to the public to
serve only the recovery workers, he thought proudly of
young Ralph, his friend who played the viola in a string
quartet, now organizing daily concerts in the chapel. Then
he pictured George Washington's pew, and in his mind, he
heard hardhats singing God bless America
The steelworkers who built the towers
                            Volunteers   heroes In the rubble
                            How different now
                            To feel their patriotic pride
                                My answering rush of patriotism
Too much patriotism?
May 8, 1970. He remembered the hardhats from the
construction singing God Bless America as they marched to
break up the Peace demonstration on Wall Street
                            The attack
                                    Flower Children
Wounded children

9/11
tragedy brings us together
                            Calls: Were we all right?
Barry & Jane in Toronto
Tony in Perth
Dagmar & Jochem in Frankfurt
Geri in Columbia Falls

" I've never been there, but I got sick to my stomach when I
saw what happened." — Harris, the young lobsterman on
Beals Island.
Hamilton thought of the candlelight service in Maine
outside the old Columbia Falls town hall, all the
townspeople holding US flags and singing God Bless
America and praying together and holding hands and

tearfully embracing in horror & hope
                    UNITED WE STAND
He thought of the little flags in his window box and the
dashboard of his car and the main street of Columbia Falls
lined with flags and the simple Godly patriotism of its
people.

He took the N train home. All talk in the crowded subway
car ceased when they went past the World Trade Center stop
slowly without stopping.

Day 49
October 29, 2001
News: NASDAQ Considers Moving Office from 1 Liberty
Plaza.
Hamilton sat on a black stone flower border ledge outside
the building.
They won't move.

He took the paperback Qur'an out of his jacket pocket and
flipped through it, looking for the passage about the virgins
promised to jihad warriors. He admired the beautiful Arabic
letters of the text accompanying the translation.
            Surah 37
"Allah has begotten children?"
            What is the matter with you?
They should be more against Christians than Jews.
And again
            Surah 18
            Al Kahf (The Cave)
                He (Allah) may warn
            Those (also) who say
            "Allah has begotten a son":

No knowledge have they
Of such a thing
                        nothing
But falsehood

Hamilton flipped pages. More on Jesus:
            But he claimed not divinity: he\was
            A true servant of Allah

                        Thus will Allah say:
            O Jesus the son of Mary
            Recount my favor to thee and thy mother.
            Behold! I strengthen thee
            With the holy spirit.
            So that thou dost speak
            To the people in childhood
            And in maturity.
            Behold! I taught thee
            The Book and the Wisdom,
            The Law and the Gospel.
            And behold! Thou makest
            Out of clay, as it were,
            The figure of a bird,
            By my leave,
            And thou breathes into it,
            And it becomes a bird,
            By my leave

            "Cherisher of the worlds"

Denial   Yet respect   Honored Prophet.

Looking for the virgins
This?
Back in Surah 37: Al Saffet

Their glances, with big eyes
(Of wonder and beauty)
(Delude) eggs closely guarded
What the hell does that mean?
He continued to search.
Scholar:
In a time of jihad, when people give their all and even their
lives for the common cause, they must be accounted more
glorious

Allah has granted
A grade higher to those
Who strive and fight
With their goods and persons
Than those who sit (at home)

"A hijack religion!" Hamilton looked up to see the burly
gray-bearded man who had shouted at him in a deep
voice.
"They say Abraham was a Muslim. Moses was a Muslim.
Jesus was a Muslim. What a mishmash!" the man
continued, throwing out his heavy arms.
Hamilton shrugged feebly. "Yes?"
The big man admonished Hamilton with upraised finger:
"Each religion in the history of the world is worse than the
one that preceded it." He turned angrily and walked away.
Hamilton felt relief.

He pictured tall young Ahmed from the grocery store down
the street as a Taliban warrior. I see menace everywhere
He recalled the trip to Rome. Jesus! Flying on the day we
started bombing Afghanistan
            Margaret & me nearly missing the plane when

they made me take off my shoes.
She knew from CNN but hoped I wouldn't turn on the TV
"Relax, John. Security will be tight."
"There's no security."
"Think of the wonderful time we'll have when we get there."
"There's no security anymore, Margaret"
"Let's try to have fun, John, otherwise they've won."
A little impatient with me
"They have won."
"Only if you say so. We'll have the time of our lives."
"Nowhere is safe."
"They say all joys are sweeter under the shadow of the
sword."
"I hope so."

They enjoyed Rome. Such a romantic city.
But the hotel too close to the American Embassy. Target in
Paris
Why not a target in Rome   Surely a target
He pictured their dinners outside in the warm evenings
only a block from the embassy, recalling his persistent
nervousness. Better after a few glasses of wine
Drank more than usual.
He remembered the Roman waitress, aspiring to be a
journalist, whose best friend was killed at the World Trade
Center.
Everywhere
People wanted to talk about it
Hit home
Everywhere
Hamilton returned to the Qur'an.
                    For those who resist Allah
                    Is the penalty of the Fire.
He closed the book, intending to read more that night.

Allah El

He tried to remember an encyclopedia article on the names
of God

                                               El-Elohei

Eloha   Elohim   YHWH   Yaweh
Ilah the Arabic
From the same root
                  The same God
                  The same fire
All claim Abraham

I sing of primordial El, and El-Elohei and Ilah Allah,
The names of God in the family of Abraham,
I sing of man perplexed by God.

Day 98
December 17, 2001
Rector & Greenwich, this corner again.
"Is this Ground Zero?" the plum-shaped woman asked a
workman down in a snake pit of cables in the middle of
Rector Street.
"Yes, Ma'am. The outer perimeter." He gestured toward the
cranes amid the shards.

THUNDER LINGERIE
CLOSED

Pink awning

PUSSYCAT LOUNGE
OPEN
US flags

REMY LOUNGE
We ♥ You

147

To All Service Men and Women
POLICE ? FIREFIGHTERS
EMS ? MILITARY
2 for 1 all night long

SOPHIE'S RESTAURANT
Cuban Cuisine
CLOSED

Hamilton entered the Greenwich news store and examined
the Twin Towers calendar. He bought a Hershey bar with
almonds.
I'll regret it
       My reactive stomach
Eating two squares of chocolate, he perused the Greenwich
Jewelers window, fixating on the Twin Towers paperweight
and a tiny US flag glittering with rhinestones. Street vendors
hawked NYPD and NYFD   baseball caps and T-shirts.

He decided to go to Trinity Church. Almost like
sleepwalking
Daily life like a bad dream
The reopening of the church comforted him. He took a seat
in a middle pew. The church was almost full at 3 PM. A tour
was in progress. So many people here these days. He opened
THE BOOK OF COMMON PRAYER at random.
           The Bishop asks the candidates:
For Confirmation?   Do you reaffirm your renunciation of
evil?
He leafed through the liturgy.
        PSALM 11
        When the foundations are being destroyed
         What can the righteous do?

        Upon the wicked he shall rain
        Coals of fire and burning sulphur

And scorching wind shall be their lot
Like WTC like Afghanistan?
A rain of missiles
upon the wicked?
Or on the innocent & wicked alike
God is not great
God is not good
Hamilton was shocked by his inner voice.

PSALM 55
His speech is softer than butter,
But war is in his heart.

His words are smoother than oil,
But they are as drawn swords.
George W. Bush?
Osama bin Laden?

WAR endless war
Infinite Justice
Infinite blood
Hope
trickling away

Hamilton was tired and depressed.
Ethical progress. Hamilton believed he had witnessed
ethical progress in his own lifetime, and he had liked to
proclaim it:
War has become unthinkable as a valid instrument of
foreign policy by the civilized nations.
Threat of Nuclear Armageddon
War unthinkable
Peaceniks won

"Ain't gonna study war no more
"Ain't gonna study war no mo?"
Didn't they sing no mo? Pete Seeger? Woody Guthrie? I'm
really out of it.
Test Ban Treaties Nuclear Arms Treaties United Nations
Humanitarian Missions The War on Poverty Pax
Americana

Back to war.
Infinite Justice The War on Terror

Biological weapons
ANTHRAX
Smallpox?

'AL QUEDA NETWORK DESTROYED'
Hamilton was skeptical about the claim. He thought he
knew why the opposition had evaporated. The Qur'an
taught that Muslims when in foreign lands or facing
overwhelming force need not observe the usual rules of   the
religion openly, nor wear their traditional garb, but   blend
in with the surrounding population instead.
                              Biding their time   Waiting to strike
another time
He opened the Qur'an again.
                    Fight in the way of Allah
                    Against those who fight
                    Against you but begin
Not hostilities. Lo! Allah
Loveth not aggressors. And
Slay them wherever ye find
Them and drive them out of the
Place whence they drove you out,
For persecution is worse than slaughter.
?? mixed message

He turned back to The Book of Common Prayer.
Surely
Thousands fold
Against the wicked
He thought of bombs. Smart bombs   Daisycutters Allah
bombs
Surreal.
Surreal: the word so often used for 9/11
Surreal: the bin Laden family and George Bush Sr. in
business together in the Carlyle Group investing in war
machines
the Bradley Fighting Vehicle the Battle Command Vehicle
the M4 Command & Control Vehicle the Grizzly the
Armored Gun System the Electric Gun/Pulse Power
technology the M6 Linebacker the Paladin the Crusader
the et cetera et cetera
United Defense   Making billions
Infinite Amorality
If fiction, it would be unbelievable.
He found himself reciting the Lord's Prayer. When he
finished, he remembered that his friend Dovid, the scholar,
told him that the Lord's Prayer and the Kaddish   were
virtually identical in the original Aramaic.
Looking through the prayer book, he again took offense at
the revised ritual. The old Episcopalian liturgy had
language reminiscent of the King James Bible, more
poetic.

He browsed through the Communion ritual. If God is
listening, he won't be impressed. It won't work.
             and although we are unworthy
             through our manifold sins
             to offer Thee our sacrifice,
             yet we beseech Thee to accept
             this our bounden duty and sacrifice
             not weighing our merits,
             but pardoning our offenses

Off the hook so easy?
By habit, he attended church when it was convenient, and
accepted Communion, although he had stopped
believing in the group confession. Sometimes he felt as if a
Divine Power worked in the universe. More often he
doubted.
Hamilton prayed:

>   Have mercy upon us.
>   Grant us Thy peace.

He felt as if the very wish for peace had power.
God or no God
Peace life love

>   The quivering of life
>   Who said that? Anyone?
>   The quivering
>   Of

No   Yes   life
quivering
O a critic
            Irving Howe   quivering reality

Should I have been a professor of English literature?
He had yielded to his father's wishes.
The law. The family tradition   the money

How I loved Shelley
He tried to recapture Shelley's The Revolt of Islam. Relevant?
All he could remember was a quote from the poet's preface.
Love is celebrated everywhere as the sole law which shall
govern the moral world.
Moral world?
Love
      Love Life
Shelley's last poem
                The Triumph of Life
Can life triumph?

The man was uncertain and afraid. Discretely, he wiped away a few tears before leaving Trinity Church.

The quivering of life, I sing, and the law of love.
I will the triumph of love, as love is life.

Eric
Greinke
(1948 -   )

Uses projective techniques to synthesize universal images into ambiguous, non-linear sequences to represent shifting perceptual fields, in an attempt to explicate the ineffable spiritual & emotional spaces between persons & objects.

THE BROKEN LOCK

1.

The Chevrolet beneath the seaweed
Resembles, say, a pendulum.
In the glacial sewers
They all look like abandoned books.
They gather in fields of blood.
They wait another minute.
Falling faces scrape sharp edges
Against us as we watch the stars.
Our marching machine begins to fill with foam.
Our slowly cracking table says "Goodbye."

2.

In the prison of the glossy blanket
Strangled paper cars claw in
Sober luxury. Handgun. Caress.
Membrane. Attempt. A silver
Tunnel carves an orphan
Illustration on our fragile female
Hatchet. A tiny cutlet
Whirls in nude simplicity. Our magnet
Signs the blank, transparent
Mortgage of the jealous cartoon.

3.

We take the tapered candles past
A nest of burnt-out lightbulbs. We
Shake our messy napkins in the
Trans-Atlantic air. Our teeth
Are scared. Our hands are
Running in front of
Speeding snake bracelets. We
Have lost our shoes! We
Have lost our season tickets! We
Have lost our fried potatoes!

4.
A placenta of noise
Masturbates in the ambiguous
Bandshell. Car-pool. Vendetta.
Banshee. Balloon. Barrels of
Dead kittens crouch on stereo
Loading platforms. Juicy
Manikins balance on
Shrouded pedestals. Our grief is
Greater than all the porcelain in
Mexico. Our grief is a polar bear.

5.
Candy-striped plants lean toward
Windows of music. Strawberries
Buzz obsessively in the creeping
Rain. Bulldogs escape
Homosexual worms. Our
Harmonicas are leaking! Our
Underwear is illegal! Our
Grandparents are alive! Our
Rescue gear is stolen! We grease
Our feet & slip into the night.

6.
Sandwich. Beacon. Crawfish. Mistake.
Persian maids lounge in secret
Frameworks. The bells of
Mystery ring a song of strange
Graduation. Our bluebird
Reeks of soy sauce! Our bean-bag
Unfurls in hymenal splendor! We stand
On the threshold of a
Kitchen revolution! We teeter
Near the edge of an insect rebellion!

7.
Our eyes are bankrupt! Our
Noses are overparked! Our
Brains are under arrest! Our
Bones are bushwhacked! Our
Hair is ringing! Our
Legs are braided! Our
Toes are psychotic! Our
Hearts slowly stretch in the
Direction of Hudson's Bay. Meanwhile,
We hide inside a giant football.

8.
Our bed is stacked with
Grey-haired magazines, squirming
Amid discarded
Hats & umbrellas. Rusted scalpels
Litter the quaint fairground. Con
Edison. Sample. Woodcraft.
Needle. The sweet blonde
Morning declares itself. We
Inhale & hold excited breaths to
See the tortured, raving day approach.

THE RAIN

The red, orgasmic clouds
Explode sweetly above us,
Arresting dying breezes
That escape our green lungs.

Dragonfly. Maroon. Stampede. Incest.
The grey pearl moon
Incites a riot in our dreams.
Ashes rain upon the wet, enduring leaves.

WHAT TO DO NEXT

You arrive at the station
With your pockets full of time.
You're so invisible
That girls walk right through you.
Throw away your ticket
& skate away.

The clouds burn out
& ashes rain upon your head.
Your bones ache
From being used as jail bars.
Get up & move on
To the next holdup.

A dog on the coffee table!
A roller derby in the ice cream!
A piano roaring down the road!
A monkey with a gun
Has got you covered.
Keep your eyes straight ahead.

She has too much
But she wants a little more.
The room is loud
& the walls are turning brown.
Your ears are burning with old sounds.
Don't die.

Just take a deep breath,
                    get up,
                              & fly.

OCTOBER

It's 6 AM in the Universe, &
Cold. The yellow sun
Makes another dawn in the lake
Above my head. Warm blue air
Lifts the blanket from my bed.

Yesterday I wiped my father's blood
From the white cloud walls
Of my home, in another dream.

Now, awake beneath the lake, I am
Alone. The cold grey water of the lake
Invites me in, but then
I am rescued by my lover, the sun.

THE CLOUDS

A silver weed grows
beneath the footprint
of a mink. Monks walk
at dusk among the bells.

Blue apples
appear dazed in sorrow. A bat
flies from its cave
on the moon.

Green clouds rise in my mouth.

LOVE GLOVES
for Ben Tibbs

Birds flutter through his hands. He's
Histrionic, sympathetic, empathetic,
Never cluttered, nor apathetic.
He's been clever. He's some lover! He's
My father & my brother. Zen
Icecream koans advertize
His tender metal lives.
Surreal science is his triumphant plan.
Mystical alliances canonize his monumental plight:
His fingers walk the pages of delight.
His feet tiptoe the earth with bombastic pleasure.
Apple blossoms rain on him forever.

He plans his moves. He butters his words.
His hands massage the sky of love like birds.

THE STORM

Birdwomen ride rainbow bicycles
Through flannel forests.
Sirens haunt the coast.

Fish fly from the lake,
Circle, & fall dead.

Anvils of the night ring.
Clouds reflect the sea.
Bones orgy incestuously.

Arms break from the ground
In hurricanes of song.

THE CRYSTAL MUMMY

The crystal princess wakes from the stomach of the pyramid & rises straight through the ancient bricks. She hovers in the light above the peak, shining transparent & green. An anthropology professor sees the apparition & screams. The sound breaks her body into fragments that fall on the pyramid, shattering, glittering, laughing.

THE CLOWN CHOIR

The choir loft was filled with an awful quacking, as if ducks. But it was the Clowns. Their new identity.

When they were in a church, they quacked. When in a bar, they barked like dogs. In courtrooms all across the land there was mayhem - caused by the Clowns, chirping like parakeets.

A reporter asked them why they did it. They could only meow. Finally, doctors examined them.

When the exams were over, neither the doctors nor the Clowns could do anything but moo.

SEA CHANGE

Clouds are laughing. Rain is ending. The old clown sits in revery. Later, a tornado rearranged his priorities. Now, he has a line of sight to the ocean, but his gaze is inward, toward humility.

OLD WOMAN'S DREAM

I went into the garden to pick flowers, saw a rock & went to pick it up. It was a music box. When I opened it, there were three little women: one in a rocking chair, one sewing & one reading.

In the box there was jewelry & foreign money. The women said it was mine for finding it.

I asked them if I could get them anything to drink, & went in for water & an eye dropper. They thanked me & said they were human by day, but at night they became moths.

They asked me to leave the window open a little so they could come out of the rain & snow.

THE DOOR

I was sleeping on the ocean when the giant green eyeball began to raise me up, out, away from land & water, toward itself: the green eye staring through me. Feeling holy, I had to laugh. Molecules & atoms of myself were breaking apart & at the eyeball.

Absence wrapped around me as I entered the eye. I passed through with a wink & floated with no movement in the full nothing that was me & none of anything around what had been me.

There was everything like no sense of time, the way I'd always thought there wasn't.

Ever, I knew where I was: at home, standing inside my mirror, looking out at no one, looking back like me, looking.

164

I watched me for no time, infinitely wondering why I didn't think I looked like me, since I seemed to think I did.

I became a skeleton, explaining my diet to a crowd: "I eat birds, fish, animals." I was grinning. "Human flesh." I added.

My grin spread & I saw I was a priest, telling a riddle to a congregation of iron faces. My collar tightened, until I was decapitated. The congregation was water. I rolled on the floor, still speaking, still divided & connected.

My head rolled fast & motionless. It was a huge microscopic eyeball in space. I looked into my eyes. I saw a four-way mirror, with myself standing on every side, looking.

My eyes were backing away. There was a splash. I was sinking, back, into the heights of the ocean, staring away from, into & out of my eyes.

THE FACE

The sky was bright pink & an infinity of colored butterflies flashed continually before our eyes. The leaves of ice & frosted glass swam dramatically above the silent gravestones.

The tomb of the ancient soldier opened, & the image of an owl escaped into the abundant air.

A cloud of smoke revealed a thin, nervous countenance.

THE FOREST

Here there are many black trees: gnarled non-conformists, each scarred differently, each with its own concerns, own silences.

In spring the seedlings pop, pushing through the birth-wet dirt, thirsting for the life of light, straining thin arms toward rain. Many never make it through the membrane of leaves.

Some grow straight, assisted by the sun. Their lives will be tall & easy, a race for the blue ceiling. Others will be left below, imprisoned by the darkness of a taller shadow. This was meant to be. A life of desperation for some.

Here there are many still logs: corpses lying silently amid the turmoil of the new generation. Their influence is felt. Where they rest a seedling cannot break.

MASKS

1.
Clouds of joy rain painfully
On toy villages, temporarily ephemeral

Feeble trees emit intermittent screams
Samples of noise impregnate imperviously

A mouthful of antique coins
An earful of 3rd degree love

Shoreline tents, leopard skinned
Starlight on pink steel bridges

Inspirational bloodbuckets
Strain the concerts, emphatic

2.
Cockroaches, successful in longevity
Raise the standard of experience

Neurotic beasts cry bitterly
On beaches of plastic popcorn

Boxes of big dreams are filed
In hope chests & sour trunks

A surrender is signed
In 4/4 time, appalling

Alternative habits, none feasible
Mask a blatant truth, shameful

3.
Blue heron stalks motionless
Spear marks appear anonymously

Another ridiculous brainstorm
More mirth, defective but elastic

A strategic withdrawal, brave friend
Neglected correspondence, indignant

But wisely alone, inventive
Powerful, mercilessly noble

Dealers imagine victories
Over those who starve, gold-toothed

DESIRE

1: SKIN CANALS
Snakes fly toward the sun
Elements form a grammar

Spherical bodies rotate in space
Hollow noise of surf is heard

A game of hide & seek began
Round stones rose from sand

A stranger ran, hammer in hand
Against the mountains of the sun

A connection between snakes & men
A legend in the tiny islands

2: AFTER THE ROBBERY
Searchers return, bereft
Armed in suits of platinum

Even if the coffins were illusions
War broke out among the ruins

A crocodile lost its way
East or west to a fixed position

The stranger came again to play
Available in this space age

Refugees, constricted, extricate
In inexplicable picturesque epics

3: MAD MOUNTAINS
Solid stone broke the diamond saw
An iridescent surface had been formed

Departure gyrated a gentle beat
Teenagers brought the fresh roots

Without warning, there's the ruins
You find no steps, nor stairs

Consorted shapes were formed
Four balls dangled like musical notes

Gas sends out a beam of light
Sure to appear as simple ornamentation

MORNING

Birds' hearts flutter
Through roots
That drink the sky.

The autistic moon
Turns away
From moths that scrape
Fragile wings
Against its shoulders.

Worms tunnel deeper
Toward the heart
Of the sleeper.

SPACES

1. THE VOID
Ornamental bones
Climb ladders of disaster

A hot breeze laughs
Always wild & welcome

Perpetual pinpricks
Maintain their eternal courses

Shadows vanish in the night
Nothing in the mirror but light

I walk toward ruin
Guided only by the moon

2. OLD PENNIES
Many men remain mad
At Descartes, who split

Kierkegaard took a flying leap
Camus sank a camouflaged canoe

Nietzsche growled into the mirror
Jean Paul Sartre played it smart

Tzara took off his tiara
Blake jumped in the lake

Army surplus tanks
Shoot blanks into the banks

3. WILDERNESS HOTEL
A loud act of love
Shakes the foundation

Falling trees scream freely
Abandoned avenues echo no more

An egg, emotionally crushed
No one gets the joke

A van vanishes down a long road
A sound drowns in silence

We reserve our opinions
Our private parking spaces

THE MOMENT

The ocean splashed
Over the rocks
While trees exploded
Along the dusty path

An instant of sunlight
Illuminated the cedars
As seagulls dipped
Above the wilderness of waves

At the edge of the beach
A fir tree tried to sleep
While greedy green weeds
Played a cool jazz beat

An old clown collapsed
Inside the silence of his mask

THE LIGHT

1.
In a strange, low voice
In the middle of the winter

It is mandatory to deceive
It makes us want to leave

Like an old hammer on the bench
Like people drunk in a dream

My shoes are covered with dust
My tactics are confusing

Someone is always leaving
Someone else covers up the crimes

2.
The rain is the key
The dolls are asleep

There are books in the field
There are boxes of pain

This is where I see it
This light, this sleep, this touch

This is where you dropped it
This memory, this vision of wind

We must make plans
We see the victims, hear their songs

3.
Someone arrived late for
Someone else, who died

Someone came in, afraid that
Someone horrible hid outside

Like a box of raisins, spilled
Like pebbles on the beach

My imaginary range astonishes
My imaginary audience

You dropped the book, picked up the key
You put the dolls to sleep, put out the light

THE SOUND
for Robert Bly

Are you listening?
I am here.
Do you hear me burn?

Difficult
To hear me
In classes, or on buses.

But listen,
I am here
In a blind man's tears.

What is
That stealthy breathing?
The wind inside the dead.

SEARCH & RESCUE

1.
Supersonic horseshoes whiz
Past barbecued executives

Molten doughboys push their buns
Through networks of static tranquilizers

Whole blood on special sale
Blue bunnies have found the eggs

A hawk sails symbolically, hunting
Friendly chickadees, happy in morning sunlight

Loud, obvious spaces blurt out
Streams of angry money, accusing

2.
Grey morning clouds over the straits
Blue noise lights the sky

Old men follow without desire
Wildfires race each day to play

Sweet pine fragrance, crisp A.M. air
A loud chunk of chocolate breaks off

Shrill politicians whittle down the branches
Deer bed down for the day, afraid

Many of the hardest games
Were never played, until that day

3.
In the candy penitentiary
In the bloody popcorn theater

After the backward horse race
Often, but not always, predictable

On a distant planet, light years away
On top of Old Smoky, coughing

When all the trees are dormant
Barricades no one can pass

All masks removed at last
Big pike glide between lilies, predatory

SONNET IN D MINOR

A kiss echoed
Shining & clear
Across the street
Classically villainous
Wounded animals hide
In the ecstatic jungle
They do not believe
In mirrors
Fur like onyx
Black vibrations
Against exuberant leaves
In cold sunlight
A spinning frenzy
A loud caress

175

ISLA MORTE

Fallen leaves bury
Surrounding memory
Flooded
Shoreline endures
Gentle passage
Yellow roses burn
Frail chickadees
In shadows of trees
Shiver in their sleep
Space to breathe
Other lights
Answer
Human faces
Naked outcasts

LEELANAU FIRE

The night is white.
The moon, a cosmic smile.
Big wind frightens a fawn.
A branch falls, an alarm.

For awhile, I remember
Pictures across the river,
A life boat in the snow,
Radio squawking at the stars.

Now images are gone.
Mind empty, I'm alone.
Right here, by the smoke
Of the glowing embers,
Camping on the edge
Of the open sky.

MEMORY

I wake, in Civil War,
Play endless games
Of solitaire. I die,
& am reborn. I breathe,
Until my breath is torn
By unexpected stare or look
In mirror, sudden laugh
Or uninvited tear. No one knows
How slowly I have grown. No one
Knows the feelings I alone
Have given skin & bone, to float like ghosts
Past shadows of the piers & reefs, then
Rise on bells to walk asleep
Through burning cities of white peace,
Where green dreams bloom
On the pastures & plains
Of my newly wounded hands.

MOVING ON
for Ronnie Lane

The walls bear weight
Until they break. Drainpipes
Crack, & flood the wounded fields.

Rotten apples fall from neglected trees.
Tall winds rip off limbs, but
The crippled shapes still get new leaves.

You walk the roadmap on your hand,
& wake, among friends,
In a foreign land.

DUST

Obnoxious cosmetics
Drip from the face
Of the Statue of Liberty.

Diamonds gleam
From the President's teeth.

Old dogs argue
Over the skulls
Of rock stais & senators.

A battalion of metal roaches
Dances around a captured flag.

In the middle
Of the moonless night
Old men remember the Third Reich.

Alarms ring in gladiolas,
Cueballing yet another Spring.

John
Keene
(1965 -   )

Employs a variety of texual, conceptual, rhythmic
& rhetorical devices to create jazzlike pieces
from his experiences. Through shifting points of
view & voices, he reveals nuances of meaning
that transcend the everyday.

IONISATION

Yardbird drops to the sofa in a tonal haze.
Edgard leans in, his rug-lined study on Sullivan
steeping: mid-July. Ink veins his shirtsleeves,
his mind leaping with an arrangement
of percussive possibilities. The Baroness,
dragging on a bidi, asks Charlie whether Chan
can hear a pin drop when he solos as she can.
Or could: she is already losing her upper register.
Edgard, silent, could answer that perception
consists in orders of mastery. So as with genius.
The hardest art, Parker's, appears effortless.
Louise enters with a tray of tea
and salmon sandwiches, returns to her translations.
Mon semblable, mon frère....
What is the phrase that Parker is mumbling?
Black figures ambling across a snow-
jazzed... - no, no, mon ami - notes:
he wants to learn how to read them.
Edgard considers this proposition,
given that gifts such as Parker's
can hardly be set down on paper.
Where to begin? Wielding his score
of "Amériques" before the afternoon's pale bars,
his thoughts hop from scale to scale,
losing Bird to a swallow of Waller
that nests in his consciousness. Ablaze
with boredom, the Baroness rises and departs,
later denies this scene ever took place.
Louise continues casting her net upon
a French sea, hearing Parker's sweet
assents that sound like moans, her husband's
faltering voice, the ever-confident
pianoforte: *I is another*

UNTITLED (MOTICOS: RAY JOHNSON)

Question: "The black singer....?

Antarctican
bunnyheads
cove(r)
dear Josef Albers,
Eskimos (not quite it)
Feigen Gallery
gasoline
hat (black)
"isolated"
January 13
kill (do not)
Lucky Strike
mountain (black)
nothings
osmotics
postage
Queen's fingernails
ray(on)
silhouettes
throwaways (tender buttons)
urinating
Venetian (blind-like effect)
Water (Street)
xerography
yellow circle
Zoroastrian (Norman Solomon)

Answer: "...Al Green."

TEN THINGS I DO EVERYDAY
after Ted Berrigan

Floss my throat
                  wash my feet then glower
kiss Curtis at 7:30
                to shake him
feed Kitty
         philosophical tenders
stroll the valley
               of dearth to Journal Square
keep the faith like a Benedictine
                    under the Hudson

Work like a yoyo
                nap like bear
address endless e-mails
             to forgotten writers
jack the meter
     to stand tall
drink lust as if
             it were spring water
walk through the Mews
        when the coast is near
leave my friends and shadows
             generous margins for error

DARK TO THEMSELVES

Invent, experiment: chaos
that doesn't swing but dances tight

as a drumhead so taut it might
explode: whole notes cleaved

183

into sixteenths with a single blow, melodies
receded as arpeggios. *Say, what he call this*

composition? Tiny fingers divining
an architectonic flow, forearms jacking

cracks in the keyboard as wire
and wood cry out in agony:

duo enter, ringing changes.
Liberate the dissonance without killing

the blues. Unit structure: cut it.
They don't teach this joint in the Conservatory.

Varèse via Jelly Roll, serial Waller,
harmony ribbons in a Möbius strip.   Recut it.

Enough is enough. *Brother can't play
here no more, the customers ain't paying.*

Even Miles was giggling in the darkness.
It's always a bitch to be out

front. He summons the baseline
of his thoughts in the shadows, tracing a new theory

of silence. Don't worry about the next gig.
Their ears are still learning.

"INBETWEENNESS' (MORTON FELDMAN)

```
Lower                                    (Lower )
        Now drop it
                    lower still.
                            still more
                slowly
        till the interplaying
                of the bows bores
                                deeper channels
                        in the inner ear
                                    traces
            of an F-train's
                        after-roar
                        or laughter fading
        from far corners
                    of a Brooklyn
            roller rink.
                        white whispers
                flickering in legato
    across the dark
                concreted bowl
            of Washington Square
                            (echoes after stumbling
            from the Cedar Bar
                        at closing ) Machines.
                            sighs. parting thighs.
                        graph paper crumbled.
            a cigar's embers,
                        rug weave patterns tracing
            a dying scream
                            (How many more
            hours before
                        the quartet downshifts
                            into silence') By then
    the agony of so much
                    pleasure has perforated
            memory. redefined
                    the yawning gulf between
        suffering and joy.
                    between the persistence
                                of dead systems
                        and music's
            lyric revolt.
                    Anxiety and endurance: Were you
    listening' Did it
                        hurt you? Can you remember
            it and if you can
                        how will you
                                put it together
                        this time. recombine
                    each exquisite note
                                and line'?
```

THE ANGEL OF DESOLATION

The Angel of Desolation appears one Sunday evening only a few hours after we have gotten back from services. Mid-June, and everyone is sporting summer-weight suits, listening to the gospel CD calling out ecstatically in the background. We are playing bid whist, drinking Seven-and-Sevens, talking above the music as if we had never talked before in all our lives. Someone - I can't recall - is gossiping about some man who was tipping with another brother's man while his own man was wailing for him at home, and who - now he means the first man - when he found out what was going down, showed up at this other brother's - this is the last's one's - job with a revolver and an ultimatum.... I sigh, because I've already heard this story twice before.

The Angel of Desolation, a friend of somebody's friend, enters the room with little fanfare, making sure he catches my attention. After he politely removes his fedora and slides into a chair beside me, he says his name in a Delta accent so softly that I can barely hear him. It's as if he's revealing an embarrassment or a secret. He's not flashy, despite the gold pinkie ring and the slightly-thicker-than-modest chains spilling onto his immaculate shirt, or the crown that glitters in his mouth like a beacon. Truth be told he's so quiet, so unassuming, no one else seems to know he's here. Dressed in a tan gabardine three-piece suit and spit-shined brown Stacy-Adamses, he naturally volunteers to be my partner when it's my turn to play- Sure, there is something forlorn about him. Yet he plays his grief so close to his vest that I nearly miss it. Now he is humming a hymn I recall from childhood, that they rarely if ever play in this church I go to now.

See, the Angel of Desolation is playing his trumps. He's obviously guessed my particulars. He knows that I'm a sucker for gabardine and patent leather, for hands as large as somebody's daddy's. He knows I have a soft spot for men who show a little too much gold, who lack for taste but not for modesty. He's figured out somehow that I have a thing for folks who carry the country everywhere with them, who know how to beguile by invoking subtly a childhood they have never really known- We trade smiles, and, after lightly touching my knee, he dons his hat. There is something terrible I'm sure he wants to tell me, but I don't press him, and being gracious he holds back for now. The Angel of Desolation leads me to the front door, where I offer our goodbyes. The music doesn't break, I don't turn back.

Funny no one notices we are gone.

KLEIN BOTTLE

But *this is not a klein bottle*
its surfaces multiply bounded
observation displays distinct clusters
distributes its modes of reference
figures emancipated as organized
differentiated perceptual color space
into notatable architextures
describe and draw the mechanics
of the mapping function fracture
by exploring a nervous system
described through graphic algebra
dispersal molded in each seam
its stimuli and seismic models
the global represents the possible
range of subjects and objects
but this is not a klein bottle

CHAMBER CINEMA

beneath your iris or fundamental variable
  beneath your world and its referent response
I lift it however I peer in, entering
    current and extension
    reminded of drafts I
have seen, a tension of spiral, extending
  sensation into line tone time and rhythm
mark architecture
  attentive to the physical conversation
    I am behind an oscillating
psychic screen
  the scene of the act,
    envisioning beauty and its planar articulation
I am in your chamber cinema
  below root imaginary, a dialogue exposed
in which becoming will
  breathe, think, live, work, cry, crap, die
    but track free play of dreams
and distill them
to their furthest extremes as dreams and symbolic expression
    pairing
contraries on which they lie
    still within
    condition, how tactile relevance holds system and
ethic
  within cohesion, the conversation
    of finger and iris physicality or deflection
  straight but close, from distance
    and reflective vantage
soul seethes and shifts
  the improvisatory pleasure
    of making
drawing seeds
  recedes

PROPOSITIONS

if p	then perception
reducing surface	physical responses
fragments	hinge
cartographies float	against finality
clouding	layers
on paper slope	light-intensity and action
map compositional	signal levels
serpentine patterns	trap
as momenta	charts of identity
if conception	*then p*

GEODESY

invisible	skin	shatters	manual	diffusion
machine	merges	psychic	sub-planar	tears
node	bounding	shadows	subjective	dynamics
serpentine	prisms	refract	metaphor	consciousness
interior	wave	curtaining	seismic	effect
billowing	perforation	spans	metamorphic	position

REFLEX

Memory's borders turn, always returning. In the return, what is dissonant binds them. What they resist they harbor. What they ignore they engage as a deeper synthesis. The images strive but cannot depict this surface. The omitted returns strengthened, returns and replicates its diffusion throughout all layers. In the image, in the mirror the intimate boundaries erode. Held. The erasure stains. In the return, the repressed is energy, is loosed as the eyes' or pen's method of addition. Constraint releases faltering resonances. Lost: every loss upends memory. Leave the edges and nothing adjourns. Lost trains of images return. Marked, the journey from point to point begins, lengthens in the imaginary plane. In the disappearance, the intimate nests. Abstraction: departure is no haven, the passed over transposes and holds fast, moored. The dissonant refrains, the trembling loss, puncture memory's borders. What was cast away retains its power: stain.

PRISMS

attack motion

less mathematical than lyrical

effort notation

iconographic force

private ghosts dialogue

catching scribble

exploratory forums

Richter echo

breathing thinking

emotional event in mark

emanating splendor

by sensograph and eye

pictorial storms

x-raying concept

190

ideational response

communicating mind as line

shear interiors

constellation sharing

MAP

interior motion realised shatters contiguow fragments

visualization: as photic: all possible: sensate momenta:

adhere or cohere in tile ideograms representing multiple

present motive: ideogrammar: lapping over

valued frictions emotion scatters perceptual sheets

repeat each: valuated functions: represent exploratory

overlap into interpretive graph responses

glyphs: meaning hives: diagrams blend: knot ambiguities:

flow in surface tactile configurations threading

dynamic waves: cut across: invisible: root figurations:

different material series public tranverse

sublimate: fuse difference: creating: local iconomies

interconnections visualized motives shatter

material: rows to shifts: general level: signals:

complex plane realize surface upheaval

complexity phrasing: retinal syntax: drawn in: common:

inflected cartographies pressed to arc and line

event zones: by line: or rift: echo locations: drafting

bear other potentialities through bundled junctions

sensations converge: through bodily: sentience passage:

dialectic eruptions as discontinuous subjects

carry: mode narratives: every hollow: system radices

dialogues rendered in numinous fragment designs

space housing: perceptual stages: dialectic structures

LOVE WAVES

Shuttle never still but wander. Intensity drums in coils. As from a river, a field, as love waves, spirals darking at angles where concept begins. No sparks but marking where intent and content part. Simulations. Signs flicker, stimulating the stylus to record upper and lower registers. Once I asked what they captured and I still wonder. In the marks, nothing staffs and nothing falters, recesses fill and fade away. In their wake, subject. Wandering in tight arcs which compiled process as shimmering lattices, the gestalt trajectories. Models combine. Does definition point to moments where each image ravels? In dense expressions, the intersecting planes augur structure.

Once presented as seismic clusters of negative light, black and whiter black, wavering knots. Within light, in grooves, what coils there? The traveling velleites folding, vibrating unto themselves. Like phases in a shuttle they spin and drum. I asked of these shimmering lattices, salvaging nets spun out from the thrumming, these last shaped, seismographs? Never still their notation - revolution.

TRY TO REMEMBER THAT SOUTH AFRICAN MAN

Sometimes I try to remember the name of that South African man, who insisted on being called "Coloured," even though in this country he would have qualified as "black " He was more attached to that identification than any other, such as "older," "dapper," "tourist," "uncut," "speaks Afrikaans," "wears glasses." His hair ran under my fingers like lambswool; he could tongue longer than any guy I'm come across thus far. What did we talk about as we lay on The comforter in his hotel room? Getting around Boston on foot. How we'd both considered studying architecture. Apartheid over there, racism here, especially how Black Americans had achieved so much in comparison, how we seemed to take everything for granted. Back and forth Imagine if just bitching about inadequate schools and lack of housing could land you at the bottom of a ditch, he asked me But it happens here too, I protested. He smiled: I know, respect your elders, even if they're lovers. Be quiet, now, and then his palm covered my mouth and nose, leaving a small slit for me to breathe. This is how they held me before they began to beat me, he said. Then he showered me with another round of kisses.

AFTER C(2): DIALOGUE

In such space
           MASS
To S. marks like PHALLUS
                    and its attendant forms
                how the negative detaches
                    in its consciousness
      KNOTTINGS
           spontaneous filament of course
                              CLOUD
                attempts to picture beyond natures
Rendering configurations as shown,
                    drawn through the required differings
      strewn full of abstraction like
TIME   or
      GASES.
Over both, no greater FLOWS
                    or STARS,
                primary, no other
                    course but to hold and mark them
                              making
from the mind's HEART, from GRASP
      and FEAR and LUST
                come subjects.
BREATH, HUNGER, CLITORIS, IRIS
                When drawn, however, the unnatured
      is a SCREEN made up
                of its component patterns. The (un)
in universal COURSES.
                AIR wells into HAIR, diagrams
      form and require control
                MATTER bargains attraction.
      TEXT-
ure endures.
To S: YOU are

194

wholly of the DRAWING
THINGS, constellate
selves
making
unMASKS
marking
MANifests

FUGUES

With two fugues, multiply positions. To illustrate the idea, model, then gestural. First fugue subject: the image to be charted. Second fugue subject: improvisation. A lover, a park, a neighborhood street recalled, figures improvised from generalized scenes and cityscapes you the viewer live in. First fugue subject: polyrhythms. Second fugue subject: encounter. Two positions codified in gesture, where the presentations in indigo ink and pencil cluster. Where the eyes trap a series of lines and swirls, you orchestrate violent transitions through which the idea can be opened. Part polygon, part sphere, by diagramming opening. First fugue subject: modal. Second fugue subject: stretti. Models, aHare presented as nearly flat on both sides, representing scales and places that emerge from engaging boundaries. Imagine trajectories. Formally, any object abstracted or stored indexes your imaginary. Creating through superposition of themes and tropic rhythms: where deferral becomes an art of witnessing.

OSCILLATION

visible	topoi	echoing	spiral	delay
density	sets	merge	coupling	symmetries
rapturous	boundary	graphing	subjective	technique
interior	threading	transitory	labyrinthine	cartography
faultline	rhythm	signals	lyric	plenitude

195

SLOPE

against scatter	binary code
intermittent seismic	networks
in Austria	k is used
graphite slides in	waves of elasticity
joints elide	intercept form
recorded slopes'	at nexus note
is it ecstasy	not known why
path and node	sectors
pattern arrival	against stasis

COMPOSITION

From many sources,
       dissolution, many
              voices: vision. When searching
       at the edge of self what is the source
of method, outside, the limit?
                     Driving at what is arriving,
              you must parse it out.
       Runs, parallels, a configuration
              of plane, point, volume
                     relations: across
              the initatory continuum between
                     palm and performance,

desire stages: release
                      pleasure, draw it.
      Highway of personal shadows
    and yesterdays,
                  the intimate summoning
byway with its unfathomable brightness.
    What does the image stammer
                    if you listen
carefully? Part of it is surprise,
           reflects the terrifying
   or sublime coming under, freeing as in
an mnemonic dissonance
      or narrating others' forgotten
sexes, variables. Even tedium,
      repetitive delirium. Parting,
so you empty and it becomes
           yours - you. Another
     is rigor that roils
               about the idea
        core. I - when I am others
       inside myself,
                   eyes at the various
    levels so I touch and embrace
       new and luminous eruptions -
    I - what we are deriving
      from this graphite
facility, dark networks
      of imaginaries that project
            in each hatch?
From many sources, the signs
     voicing clarity
    and the risk of trying, the task
      gathering action
         inside: not complete,
   till not mine, one mind
      still in many
  the limit hard

won, bearing ecstasy - not one
        but many, undone:
redrawn: design

PERPENDICULAR

By talking through ourselves to our private margins

We are braking thinking, personal, introspective

We are linking exploratory, how to arrive at, embody lucid

We are drinking looking, or how to transcribe what eludes us

For our selves, or a chance to share and enter other ones

On sharing these, egos, eros and what slows us

By walking through this perpendicular of cloud sheave and stroke

We are leaving thinking, for expressive and physical intervals

We are layering thinking in intensity and its physical presentation

Graving in gesture the found and enfolding wave process

Breaking public messages, we who strive to form and respond

Making public modeling, rituals of the looking process

Within us transformations of structure, dynamics of impure story

Within us evolutions, reflecting wholes appropriating patterns

You, looking at thinking, uncoding referent mystery

We, deciphering hemisphere and plane we peer into, draw through

199

Lynne Savitt

(1947 -   )

Uses a stream-of-consciousness approach combined with run-on lines to evoke innerpersonal & interpersonal relationships.

After the Rape
for my son, matthew

I

When i think of those two boys,
               I see you,
an angry nine year old blaming me
                   for the men
who leave your life,
             Understanding angry boys,
             Understanding violence
             against women.
             Understanding helpless mothers.
Matthew, we cannot fault the shiny barrels, melting
bullets, the spring that snaps under pressure.
             We are all manufacturers.
When you slam your door,
                 i hear gunshots.
I am as frightened of your speedy caress
                    as I am
of those faceless boys.
After months, I still cannot go to airports.
A plane ticket to San Francisco sits on my desk.
. Matthew, I want to be able to hold you again

                    but

you are bullets blast, recoil.
Do not be angry at blondes, breasts, husbandless women.
Do not love sitting ducks.
Fight to be a moving target and escape
this shooting gallery.

****

II

George showed me how
                to load his twelve gauge
looking down those shiny barrels.

But what would I do with a shotgun in the ladies
room at the Seattle airport?
(tell your lover you've been raped; hear him
        ask if you responded)
I am now living alone
with my tiny breasted daughter, my pistol packing son
in a house by the bay
where the lights keep flashing and
the ringing bells still scream   BULLSEYE!

Writing

my friend leo says
it's okay to get
old & fat
to be remembered
as a blonde
dream carrying a rose
a pink velvet
ass bent over
a car fender
a warm mouth
wet as the tropics
all you need
to write, he says,
is the memory
he continues through
the phone wire
as you put yr

fingers under
the elastic of my
mauve lace panties
memory blazes
poems poems poems

A Day At The Beach

under your parents' roof
you become a child again
parenting the children
they've become drowning
in the thick power
of the last moments
of their arduous swim

you're in love with the towel girl
the coconut oil she carries
in her little striped beach bag
her coral toenails showing
through her brown leather sandals
make you giddy

· everything tingles with the
backstroke of passion
on the shore of death

afternoon sun & medication
transform the ordinary
into ultra poignant relays

you're always out of breath
out of sorts   patience   understanding
but not out humor or lust

intensity makes you attractive
the towel girl thinks so too
she wets your thighs with oil
for the reading of the will

your parents are calling
they want sandwiches without crust
lemonade with little umbrellas
the sound of your recognizable voice

the heat & salt water exhaust you
yr postcard reads, "sometimes wish you were here"
the towel girl licks the stamp before you mail it
summer won't last forever

On The Hospitalization of My Daughter For Diabetes

all my plans
                we cannot run
                                away now
all my plans
            for covering our nipples
                        with forest leaves
            digging our toes into the plush gray
            carpet of a san francisco apartment
            hiding out with donald duck for weeks
                        at disneyland
no one was going to be able to find us my green
                        eyed daughter
grandma, brother, your long gone father would
search the editorial offices, bookshops, readings
& we'd be in oregon, arizona, montana, idaho
& we'd be tying flowers, shells on a string

                          in our hair
all my plans
        for kissing the suntanned knees
        of old california lovers
        the knuckles of beer breath loggers
you
    the perfect daughter
you
    the perfect star
you
    the perfect

all my plans
        for the nuclear holocaust
        survival of the strongest
and you will need your insulin

all my nightmares
        a newly knit muffler
                        choking my summer spirit
i fill the syringe
i rub your perfect thigh with alcohol
oh, my perfect
oh, my plans
oh, my daughter....

Everything I Know About Life

can be summed up
in just one sentence

he forces her legs
open with his knee
and before she can
fantasize about tahiti
it's over

The Undoing Of Mrs. Lattrice

began slowly with a piercing look
how easy she crumbled his fingers
found her heart hot pulsing in her
pants pulled off so fast wet as spring
in her step strangers recounting change
her mind, her manner, her sheets
to the wind they rolled over past crime
won't help her now he owns her body's
manual flips the pages laughs naked
as old dreams slip away from any part
of herself she recognizes hungers thought
far gone as a woman ruled by a man who
knows just how far to push in push
out of her mind they are saying did
you see the buttons of her ruffled, purple
blouse left undone as a wino's fly? what will
become of mrs. lattrice now that she's
opened wide as the canals in venice? whispers
fill the air of his warm breath on her neck
makes her slide ice cubes up & down his
hard understanding controls her love
him forever she gasps, pillow over mouth
hand over eyes, blindfold over heart
slipping away she is undone

He Asked Me If I Ever Think About You

while we were sitting on the deck
watching the boats slap the water
drinking margaritas with yellow plastic
straws limes falling on my pale pink

skirt barely covering swirled gold toe
ring the memory bell & we are back at
the lake, the four of us, you, me, lulu &
tony laying in front of the fire empty beer
bottles in a green plastic bag remnants of
a picnic, potato salad in a pink ceramic bowl,
hot dog rolls in the dirt, a bag of marshmallows
next to bottle of vodka & the guns shining in
moonlight like your very blue heart i loved you
more than all the others i gave it up for that
feeling i only had with you safe as israel's army
i needed no borders it all was yours do i ever
think about you drunk car hitting an oil slick
smacking into a pole holding your gun & chain
with my ring pressed so tightly in your fist
it left a mark like you did on me the ring still
burns & they buried you with those guns cold
& hot you used to say, baby, run as hot as you
do cold day i stopped thinking about you hourly
a couple of years ago unless someone mentions
undying love or sex hot as french fry cooker guns
as objects of desire & art i dodged a bullet & will
love you as long as the water slaps the deck
sitting here drinking margaritas with yellow plastic
straws you were not the one who broke the camel's
back & sometimes i tell him i do think of you

Blizzard 2003

we came so close to levity
it was almost love
giddy with lacy snow kisses
valentines chocolates white
stuffed bear with ruby heart

209

clichés of romance cold
as thirty years can bring
you press up against my
back some icy february
nights it's enough to be

two old blood pumps reading
red crayoned cards from grand
babies we adore each other
in a new way decades ago it was

hot as july sand at jones beach
now we shovel dizzy heaps slush
lovely as cashmere comforters
lazy blue sleepy flakes of fringe

we came so close to levity
it is almost love

Prison Poem #32

"to love without role, without power plays, is revolution."
                                        -rita may brown

i drive the long, dangerous journey
you shower, put on your clean clothes
& wait for us to arrive with books,
sometimes vegetables, depending on
what we can afford this month
i wait on line with all those
other women who work to keep
home together long hours
raise children strong as the
bars in this cold prison

after we've walked through
the four electric gates
our men will enter one at
a time we'll be blossoms
soft and perfumed and
bring them coffee, honey, sandwiches
they will warm the food, set the table

in a blur stealing intimacies
i touch you touch she rubs
he sighs robbing smells textures
to last until the next visit

sometimes i bury your head
in my breasts you find
comfort me in your arms
all is well no roles

in this love, my darling
all pins have been
pulled from the grenades
no matter how long we
must wait we will
continue the revolution

Mrs. Lattrice Takes the Children Swimming

in southampton on the rocky long island sound
carrying a bushel of sand toys & sunblock
dragging the boy down the beach, the girl skips
happily white hot sun bleaches everything
looking out at the water a skier attached to a speed
boat a dark woman in a white thong greases herself
with lotion spreads the blanket down gives each

child a juicebox their little cold, dripping hands pressing
against her flesh shocks her out of the trance
she thinks THIS is real life but cannot attach nerve
endings to anything but the brooding man who
saved her lips from cajun kisses & fumbling guitar
playing fingers the children cling like seaweed
calling her to attention between her legs a salute
to vodka & air conditioning & fingers
that do not play an instrument but
can make her sing a new vibrating music
with a voice she didn't know she had

The Child Molester, The Bottle Club & Love

he couldn't hide behind the pale
antique bottles & gentle collectors
e-bay addicts & catergorizers of
glass blob tops painted labels patent
medicine poisons milk flasks the world
of glass clear & case worn as the call
telling members he was among them
unspeakable acts embossed on his record
convicted felon tiny helpless victims heart
broken parents trust bottle collectors unite
what is valuable is agreed upon innocent
children be protected criminal be outed

when he appears at a meeting glass
heroes scatter he offers his hand
you shake it become shaken experience
automatic to gladhand when one is extended
what has love to do with this child molester &
nightmare handshake that haunts you?
thirty years i have come to know you

& see through the shelves of bottles
aqua cobalt blue cloudy lavender crystal
clear that i love you isn't based on most
prized glass cylinder but worth of what
we know is flawed & make our most
cherished of all you show as beauty
& strength real love, my glass prince, is
based on accepting what is weak & loving
what is ugly unforgiving we are to the felon
generous accepting to each other clinging
to whole healthy pink bodies of our grand

babies may they grow untouched by wretched
longings & never see black hearts we sometimes
show them a world of random acts of forgiveness
beautiful innocence they wear as splendid crowns

Summer 2004

the man wearing reflective orange vest
riding bicycle with tomato crate on back
rolling stones singing you can't always
get what you want when do i get what
i need you now more than ever before
you went away promised things would
get better off without me dragging along
burdens of aging, ailing parents never
gave anything but mouth flesh canyons
for comfort me tonight as i crack apart like
maryland blue crabs with mustard sauce
piles of cracked ice melting on sea
green plates tiny debris of day old love
like tuesday's halibut served on sunday
is this what we are left with, my sweet?
i do not want the blue plate special

break out the ivory linen tablecloth
polish the silver garnish this fresh
fish dish with lemon kisses & parsley
jewelry decorate my hot heart & it will
spill iodine valentines in your foamy lap

Autumn Farewell

i can only love
you as much as
i love all the others
& dear, there have been
many other than you & him
& seeing you frail beauty escapes
description when hard passion
softens like apples left on autumn
ground near where you sit soaking
sun you always loved the burn
now radiated by machine hearts
that can say goodbye can't be
broken by gentle kiss on your chemobald
head feels like pop after the last stroke
your wave weak as tea & i couldn't
wave back my wrist too rigid to banner
so long a finger puppet clutching
my cracked porcelain blue tinted
heart in a thousand tiny pieces
i cannot form the word but
i can only love you
as much as i love

Ignition

the shirtless man in the green
work pants digging in the gardens
at the arboretum
the woman carrying her wide brimmed
straw hat the breeze blowing her pink
& fuchsia flowered skirt as she walks
something in his eyes, the sweat beads
on his abdomen, something in her
eyes, the tan line on her breast
she touches the zipper on his pants
he grabs her wrist
the nerve fires light entangle
explode in the greenness
of their one-time fusion

i light the long slender
blue kitchen match the charcoal
presoaked in lighter fluid will flame
the very second i touch
the stick to anticipating squares

like you today on the phone
when i said, " michael, my
cunt is so hot," & i heard
your breath quicken you
answered, "say something else,
anything," but before i could
speak you came

some things are like that
the green fire of eye contact
the blue flame of the barbecue
the red heat of the phone

It's Different

now it's approaching seven
& the lines at local restaurants
are mounting you think i'll crumble
with desire to sit in a cushy booth
with warm crusty bread in a basket
running my finger down endless
selections of veal, chicken, eggplant

longing for a a slice of cheesy pizza
served on the red formica counter
icy diet coke with lemon or a margarita
guacamole salsa chips or by the water
my favorite table bloody mary shrimp
cocktail garlicky scallops salad with
goat cheese & walnuts raspberry vinaigrette

think white tablecloth a wood smoked thick
slab of steak buttery corn thai dressing
on fried calamari i love dinner out any
where drive through a few square steamed
hamburgers white castle of my dreams
our favorite pastime dining together you
think i'll crumble for the dinner hour

it's different this time i won't give in for
sustenance that never fills me i'll
gorge on dry saltless pretzels finally
acknowledging no dinner supreme or
endless with you can ever fill me
what an empty booth we fill together
does anyone know we're there?

The Transport of Grandma's Yearning Vibrator

she lives in places her pillows cannot take her
grandbabies will widen their peacock blue eyes
when she tells them about her colorful past
is a lavender balloon in the hand of a toddler
letting go as it floats towards gardenia clouds
becoming a dot on the horizon and lost mind
me, babies, live on the fringes of all your neon
nerve endings will be sweeter in a bouquet of hot
pink pinwheels sailing up to heaven's memory
filling your dreams like chocolate kisses & ether
this is a coupon to a catalog of sex toys & films,
a love note, a legacy from your maternal grandma
speaking from experience & memory's carnival

The Recidivist
for B.

how long should she have waited?
dressed in a white sequin mini dress
her long, graceful legs wrapped around
the thick, sweaty neck of a money man
the spiked heels of her boots pressing
into his armani clad shoulders

she was there when you got out that
first time hot and hopeful filled with
capricious belief in picket fences happy
endings you got into fights, feuds, drugs
even the night I was there you came home
wet running from cops hiding in a laundromat

every time you call it's a new bust,
drunk, halfway house, story the
husky, dreamy voice pulling me into
your jacuzzi eyes too full of women
i listen to the music of your movements
the smokey jazz swirling under my skirt

i thought she was perfect for you
don't want to talk about her anymore
she flew off to bimini, the bahamas, bora bora
the fluff of her streaked hair revealing diamonds
big as vegas chips dangling in her ears
the well dressed dealer, good luggage at her side

tonight when you call you tell me
any assault on a cop is a felony
you can't plead this time it's six
months sometimes before i hear from
you down in trouble searching for
breast of mother concern you get from me

she's gone and won't be back except
an occasional call late at night
when she's restless, unsatisfied
her green silk robe falling open
to lush thoughts of you fucking
her everywhere corner orifice hour

it's in you that itch that can't
be scratched that mechanical grasshopper
keeps your foot tapping, fingers drumming
all the things it takes to calm you
hurt you how long should she have
waited for you to stop spinning?

The Deployment of Love in Pineapple Twilight

camped at your tiny archway
lit by yellow glowing candles
sweet & sour as chinese pork
i taste on your full wet mouth
chopsticks red silk pajamas
slim volumes of erotica save
me intravenous they remove
from my blue swollen
hands in the midnight lime

light i call your name or name
i call your light & you appear
small screen on my anesthetized
brain me with yr club of love

where do we go now my rebuilt
pelvic paradox bops me under
wheels of progress rust like
tin cans in abandoned car
dreaming portland parables

pack yr suitcase solid meat
man of mine squeezes opal
earrings into my eighth hole
decorate depleted heart canvas

i am an artist's memory
bathing in pineapple twilight
kissing the troops of lust

Giving Up The Ghost
for a.m.

did you get the card for the memorial
our friend, noel, "celebration of a life
most thoughtfully lived" what will they
say about us i ask you as we raise
martini glasses & light a joint looking
at photos of all our old lovers eleven
boxes in the decades we've known each
other's lovers, cowboys, convicts, poets
professors, artists, mechanics, doctors,
chefs, motorcycle racers, an indian chief
& an actor we never thought this day would
come as you are to the service for once
illuminating beauty but dulled by wind &
sun mapped faces once juicy as our sex lives
now dry as feet we cream with aloe & shea
butter me up with kind words praising a life
of thoughtless pursuit & dwindling resources
oh, but the sweet memory & exaggeration of
love lies in stories bloated purple with details
how gentle & obsessed he was, how virile &
devoted our tales become classic swill but
our mirrors don't lie look at us corpses in
training big red smears for mouths never
close the coffin & sing me a dirge wrap me
in gold flecked red velvet use movie camera
to capture event I promise if you go first I'll
take the sea green tulle & sequined scallop
shells float you on a gardenia covered kayak
either way, sweet pal, don't let the legends
fade crying old lovers pulled from graves &
life to mourn us most dramatically queens
of poetry & passion may we live forever

A. D.
Winans

(1936 -)

*Addresses social attitudes & interpersonal
relationships in unadorned colloquial
language. His images are drawn from big
city streets, jazz bars & political situations,
to examine values, ethics & feelings.*

San Francisco Streets

I've walked these streets
Like a cop walks his beat
My eyes taking in her every movement
My brain storing real and imagined images
In sixty-seven years
Her changes have not eluded me
She is older now
More wrinkled and cranky
Much like me
But the two of us manage to get along
Like business partners looking out
For each other's interest
You have to learn to give and take
You have to learn to adjust
The City is like a cup of strong coffee
Stir her enough
And the flavor floats to the top

I have walked these streets
In good condition and broken down physique
Knowing there is no city like her in the world
She is like a pair of empty shoes
Sitting under the bed
With no feet big enough to fill them
She is like a squirrel running
Through the wires of a utility pole
She is like the last bullet
In the executioner's gun
She is like Billie Holiday
Drenched in Sweat
She is like the face of God
All forgiving in her insatiable lust
For life

Poem For My Grandmother

A swirling mist blows through my eyes
Filling me with strange notions
Bringing me back to my childhood
How the devil demons invaded my head
Chasing mad dinosaurs through dark alleys
Pausing to drink from my thirsty lips
All knowledge passed on down to me
By well meaning parents
Who insisted that dinosaurs didn't exist
Grandmother was eaten alive by one
She knew what I meant

Poem For My Father

I look at your picture hanging
on the wall
think back to the conversations
we never had
the way you sat there
and stared out the window
the last year before your death

no amount of drinking
can erase the memory
as I toss down one drink
after another, past soft
liver tissue, trying to avoid
the vacant look in your eyes
pieces of my brain stapled
to the lamp shade.

I Remember Still

I remember still how wonderful
it was. Running to join each
other's dreams. Sharing our separate
worlds of hope in rooms where
Angels lay.

I remember your doll house dreams
Your lips colored with flowers
My hands tracing the valley of
heaven
and finding them in your silent
curves.

It was a work of abstract art
A garden of unsurpassed beauty
I became God himself
And having you
I did not need a son.

1962

the old Black Hawk booked the
best jazz musicians of it's day
Getz, Mulligan, Diz
to name just a few

I went there but twice
once with the poet
Jack Micheline
once with a young
Latin Girl
to see Miles Davis
blow his magic

forced to sit in the
teenage section
because she was only
17
sipping on a coke
high on the high note
smoke curling around
the room in long lingering
lazy circles
sweet sax
smooth slow gin
tenor
my hand on warm thigh
feeling high
feeling cool
be-bop rhythms
dancing inside my soul

Poem For President Bush

I will not pledge allegiance
To old glory and all it stands for
The Patriot Act be damned

I will not wrap myself in your flag
And everything it no longer stand for
I will not bow down to corporate America
And its radical religious right
I will not can not accept your
Moral bankruptcy
Your green back god buying and selling
Lives on the stock market exchange

I will not bow down to a country where
Assassins determine the course of history

Whose Papal Church has its own bank
Where ka-ching ka-ching has become
The new holy mantra

America you are one big insane asylum
Your manic depressive innkeepers waging
War on the masses
Your henchmen standing proud
On your purple majestic mountains
Kissing the cold stone faces
On Mount Rushmore
Looking like a mafia don with the
Cold kiss of death on his breath

The System

There are old men and women
Who have worked all their lives
Who have put in three
Four decades for the
Right to a pension

There are old people who have
Worked twenty years or more
Only to be laid off and given
Two weeks severance pay
To seek a living
At half the pay
There are old people
Who have worked all their lives
Only to witness the company
Go belly-up
And find there is no pension
Fund left

You can find them on park benches
Or wandering sterile supermarkets
Or sitting at neighborhood bars
Nursing drinks like
A blood transfusion

They come in assorted flavors
Like "Life Savers"
Some thin and balding
Some fat and sweating
Some complaining bitterly
Some too proud to let the
Pain show
Trapped by a belief in a system
That has abandoned them

For the most part they suffer
In silence duly unnoticed
To be carted off in meat wagons
To be cut open by coroners
Who see them as morning cereal
Who go about their business
Like a butcher
Thinking of dinner
Thinking of a glass of wine
Thinking of how it used to be
How it might have been
How it should have been
It's the way of life
It's the way of politicians
And mice
It's the system where
Just trying to stay alive becomes
A small victory

Panama Memories

the young Panamanian girl
sitting alongside
her sister dressed only
in panties and bra
reading a comic book
and chewing on bubble gum
at a brothel called the
Teenage Club
waiting for the first
GI's to arrive

six girls lined-up
like bowling pins
rooted to the long
wooden bench with
zombie like stares
doing a woman's thing inside
a child's body

Bill

He keeps a photograph
Tucked away inside
His meager belongings
Three soldiers smiling
Smoking cigarettes
A Viet Cong in black
Pajamas hanging upside down
From a pole
Gutted like a fish
Flesh nailed to wood
Jesus fashion
Needs no caption

Guilt shadows him in doorways
And under freeways where
He now makes his home
Incoming artillery tears
At his nerves
Pieces of flesh stuck to bamboo
Like a piece of meat thrust
Into a tiger's cage

Vietnamese peasants
Suspected Cong
Haunt his dreams
Like a faceless Santa Clause
Leaving behind a bag
Of body parts

Ocean Beach

old ghosts stand guard at deserted
Play Land at the beach
the fat lady sings no more
the fun house torn down
like my old high school
the sand dunes filled with debris

I stare at a lone ship in the distance
the waves dashing along the shore
bringing back old memories
long buried in quicksand fog banks
my eyes a piece of dead driftwood
floating aimlessly out to sea

The Old Italians Of Aquatic Park

the old men of Aquatic Park
are dying or dead
they spend their time playing
Bocce Ball
lady death striking them down
like bowling pins

the old men of Aquatic Park
are steeped in tradition
dark skinned dressed in sport
shirts
and baggy slacks looking like bit
actors
out of a 1950 movie
dancing the last waltz on the deck
of the Titanic

the old men of Aquatic Park
sit on hard benches late in the day
their eyes taking in young women
moving left and right
as if at a tennis match
pausing to feed the pigeons
using their hands as cutting knives
to separate the crust from the
bread
which they toss into the air
like rice at an Italian wedding
rising to brush the crumbs
from their pants
one with a suit vest and tie
pulling at the gold chain holding
his pocket watch held securely
next to his heart

the old men of Aquatic Park
have the smell of garlic and pasta
embedded in their skin
Italy breathing in their heart
the old men of Aquatic Park
are dying off with grace and
dignity
and a love for the old world ways

there is something sad about
being
Americanized
there is something sad about
growing
old
the Bocce Ball rolls slowly along
the grass
coming to rest like a hearse
parked at an open grave

funerals await them
flowers scattered like empty
promises
the mourners fewer in number
their ranks depleted
file slowly into their cars
disappear into the shadows
of late afternoon monotony

Bocce Ball will resume
in the morning
there are pigeons to be fed
wine to drink stories to tell
the thirst for life masked
in the face of death

Charles Bukowski: Gods Don't Cry

He was a leper
An angel
     A barbarian.

He had shark's teeth
     That drew blood from
Friends and foes alike.

He was a shot of whiskey
A fine Cuban cigar
A rattlesnake without
A warning system.

He was a shaman
A witch doctor
A tout
A long shot in a fixed race.

He was a hit man
     Leaving a trail of blood behind
          As his signature card.

He was a geek
     A bully boy
A butterfly
A moth courting
     A light bulb.

He was a hustler
     A con artist
A defrocked priest
     Walking the streets of L.A.
          Looking for absolution.
He was a shyster

A magician
A clown with the best
            Act in town.

He was the Pied Piper
            Of Los Angeles
With a bevy of female vampires
Following him to hell.

He was the King of San Pedro
A Hollywood cult hero
Who never understood the
            Meaning of zero.

His boasted conquests
Put Don Juan to shame
Staking out his territory
Like a seasoned alley cat.

He was the undisputed champion
            Of the small press world
Taking on all comers
Ready to win at all costs
Be it by a KO or a low blow.

And he cried in the shower
But God's don't cry
Or do they?

Insomnia

Tossing
            turning
praying for sleep
when all else fails me
but God has no time

234

for insomniacs
and Christ must be busy
practicing for the resurrection

falling asleep for an hour or two
head churning buttermilk dreams
the holy ghost stopping by for a chat
seems like an amicable chap
swapping stories from the past
just as if he were one of the boys
as I gradually surrender to his will
dreams lined-up like shots
of tequila
at a Mexican brothel
only to wake again and again
insomnia a heavily armored
Spanish Conquistador
takes no prisoners
plays your mind like a card shark
your body like a whore
in the morning
leaves you feeling like bits
and pieces of a ship wreck
washed up along the shore

An Audience Of One

old songs with half forgotten lyrics
play with my head
older still movies play on the
bark of my skin
Oklahoma South Pacific West Side Story
singing on the tip of my tongue
humming my way back to yesterday
left alone with ghostly echoes

serenading the dead

I can almost feel the ignited passion
lost lovers draped on my bed
tasting the melody riding up and down
my spine

memories of my parents old victrola
vinyl records spinning
on a balanced groove
a love affair so fragile
it was like trying to thread a needle
in the teeth of a storm

fading
       fading
              fading
now like an old flame sipping
on a cup of coffee
at my favorite café
a smile on her face
fingers snapping
feet tapping to the music
that made us as one

evaporating in the face of dawn
like clouds taking foreign shapes
like the smoke rings my father
blew my way as a child
Frank Sinatra crooning in the background
the way of music
     sex
          love
               God
                    and death
playing to an audience of one.

Poem For An Imaginary Daughter

Daughter that I never had
tugging at my arm sleeve
from deaths still sleep
hanging heavy as an anchor
rooted to the tip of my tongue
your vision riding high in the
retina of my third eye

From My Window

I watch him shadow boxing
in his living room
his curtain open free admission
no questions asked
A giant Doberman
ears perched back
in attack mode watching
panting as the old man weaves
shadow boxing an imaginary opponent

From my vantage point
across the way
I watch him jab
a left hook an upper cut
and was that a Kid Gavilan
bolo punch?
Duck bob and weave
no trainer no corner man
to throw in the towel
I imagine him in the ring
bleeding out of breath
knocked down
taking the mandatory

eight count
getting back up again
beating the ten count
knowing that like the
rest of us he can't win
can't beat the odds
but refusing to throw
in the towel
nose bleeding
head pounding
jabbing punching
going the distance
hoping to get something
better than a draw

Golden Years

It's been in the thirties two nights
in a row and my heater went out
and I'm sitting here freezing my butt off
waiting for the power company
to come and fix the problem
But it isn't so bad when you consider the
earthquakes tidal waves and terrorism
that plague the universe

Thirty degree nights won't kill you
but they don't bring comfort either
The trouble with being single
The trouble with the twilight years
is knowing you could die alone
and go undiscovered for weeks
with nothing but rotting flesh
to tell your story
and a few poems to remember
you by

Untitled

torn from the womb at seven months
naked and shameless
walking Dante's world
each year a hard rainbow falling
on a thirsty landscape
the graveyard of my youth
a finely woven spider web
where unwritten words
mock unspoken vows
restless as a parting ship
with no one to wave farewell
somewhere beyond the horizon
sailors buried at sea
rise in ghostly procession
skeletons sharing their secrets
with withered old men
lined-up like bowling pins
speaking death's cold silence
measuring them limb to limb
like a tailor sizing you up
for a perfect fit

Old Warrior Of North Beach

He walks the streets of North Beach
looking like an old man
with eyes empty as a broken parking meter
Unemployable weighed down by the years
His mind heavy as an anchor
dragging the ocean floor

Forgotten rebel playing old Lorca ballads
in the shipwreck of his heart

His mind destroyed by shock treatments
and one too many police batons

At night he dreams he is riding with Geronimo
Has imaginary conversations with Charlie Parker
Rides the ferry with Coltrane and Mingus
Getting off at Bourbon Street to down
a drink with Kerouac

He shares a cigarette with Charlie Chaplin
at the old Bijou Theater
Walks the battlefields with Walt Whitman
Rides the plains with Red Cloud
in search of the last buffalo.
Walking the streets of North Beach
in search of the elusive ginger fish smell
Death a sightless chauffeur waiting
like a concubine facing another
Apocalyptic day

The Smell Of Wolves

She has a way of putting you on a downer
So that the next day is a replay
Of the Phantom Of the Opera

You hate to close your eyes at night
for fear when you wake in the morning
you will find the scratches on your back
are claw marks
and when you look in the mirror
and see no reflection
you will smell the smell of wolves
on her breath

The World's Last Rodeo

Strange this trip back in time
not with flesh and blood
but in the disguise of poems
having survived all these decades
the muscles the cells all changing dying
and yet somehow managing to survive
traveling through a strange time tunnel
through an origin you can not remember
because there is no you to remember it
walking behind my shadow
shedding the years like a snake
sheds its skin

I who have never called myself a poet
never clothed myself in consonants and vowels
nor took refuge in similes or metaphors
yet planting the words on the page
like a florist preparing a bridal bouquet
a tender arrangement of flesh and bones
at war with the demons who leave behind
a Custer massacre of words
left cooking these images like a fry cook
scrambled over easy

waking at 3 am with junkie like sweats
my eyes a heat seeking missile
honing in on an invisible kill
feeling like an alcoholic with the DT's
trying to roll a cigarette atop
a bucking bull at the world's
last rodeo

She Said Write Me A Gentle Poem

I take refuge in the gentle rain
the song of birds
the smell of spring approaching
the trees strong and sturdy bristling
bristling with leaves as I shed the years
like a lone sailor at sea charting
his way back to the womb

Doug
Holder
(1955 -   )

*Illuminates universal truths through the evocation
of minute daily particulars & memories.
He uses deceptively spare language & imagery
to confront complex emotional paradoxes.*

Harvard Square: Au Bon Pain at Dusk

You know the skids
when the "Spare Change" hawker
won't call you "young man" -
when the haunts
you slipped into
like an old shoe
are boarded
with angry wood crosses
when the glance of a beatific
Harvard girl
escapes you
with a bothered flick of her head

You sit at a table
in the court yard of the café
brittle autumnal leaves
rest,
then tumble off your round shoulders...
they just don't hold
what they use to.

It is dusk...
your knees ache clandestinely
under the table.
The prospect of sleep
awaits you
like the promise
of a young night
once did.

Morning Light In Boston

The light
drowns the beacons
from headlight
floods alleys
flushes nocturnal mysteries
from the alleys
into the street
it bleaches
the shadows
darkness
made invisible -
the winking
buildings of the
night
resume their poker face
the birds resume
their incessant conversation -
in your
wake.

The Last Smoke

And I knew better...
to flirt,
to watch
the trail
of seductive
smoke
coil
around me.
To feel -
the pleasure
the warm

fatal rush
ashes on
my breath.

What were
my gestures
without it?
Hanging languidly
from my fingers
contemplating
the ceiling -
punctuating
the before
the after,
the
hello...
good-bye.

Photo

The picture -
faded -
a yellowish tint -
"NOV. 1965"
an afterthought
on its backside.
My brother -
holding an autumnal leaf
almost a template
to his small hand.
The leaf
was brittle
with twisted veins
the rich green
the ripe bursts of color

dimmed
to a somber brown.
I remember that leaf
slipping
from his grip
with a gust
of wind
he would retrieve it...
much later.

Sig Klien's Fat Man's Shop

The sign
a flashing
fat man
clad only
in expansive
underwear
loomed outside
a rooming house window -
like a shut-in's
desperate move
of self exposure.
Comforting us
with the notion
that there is indeed
"a fit for any sized man",
just look
what's underneath.

Now My Father Can't Eat Bagels

He no longer
packs the bite
his body can't stomach it.
Somethings,
won't pass
through the ulcerated
passageway -
the sesame and poppy seeds
seek new, fertile
ground.
The lox
has made its final
run -
his sweet morning ritual
his teeth pulling
at the hot dough
his dry lips
lubricated
with a flood
of butter,
the crust cresting
at the roof
of his mouth...
its unhindered descent.

I Am A Jew

Do I have a choice?
They changed the name
trading in the awkward
Eastern European scrawl
for the short, spare efficiency -
A "JONES" is now

on my back.
This Jew
still peaks through
my body stoops
as if to "daven"
a hint of Yiddish urchin twang -
the monkish bald spot
a Yarmulke
fits perfectly.
At dusk
I down the
white bread -
secretly savor
the dark rye
and realize in
the dead of night
that the
blood
doesn't lie.

Wrestling With My Father In The Nude

Breast to Breast
he pulls me in
I break from the control
of his heavy
paternal hands.
The smell
of his sweat
a familial coat of arms -
I want to win
yet -
I need to lose,
for what can I gain?

Another King Lear
on the mat
my foot planted
on his mottled face
upright
to the
supine
there is no victory
to be had
this time.

The Love Life Of J. Edgar Hoover

The breeze crumples
your sheer caftan...
Mother downstairs
off her rocker
your loyal assistant
straddles you
and in your ecstasy
your bull dog face
creased with effeminate screams
reveling
with your little agent's
successful probe
the stiff penetration through the muck
deeper and deeper
into your stagnant well...
Reamed
clean
you sleep
with his
gentle kiss.

A Lucien Freud Nude

Her head thrown back
in abandon -
the legs like
generous thick, shanks
of beef.
The breasts -
large and flat
lay deflated
on the
corpulent folds
of her stomach.
What does she welcome?
or welcomed?
Spread
like pasty lard
on a couch
looking to the heavens
for some
piercing answer
through the
barriers
of undulating
flesh.

Concessions At Auschwitz

Yes -
these are what the tourist wants
some concession
some death camp
glass encased
air brushed -
with newly fallen snow.

The coffee table picture book,
the picturesque skeletal images
sizing up your corpse.
Or perhaps...
some boots
for a quick goosestep
around your wife -
it does so much for a marriage.
And
I'll have
two to go
well-done
but I
don't want
to taste
the ashes.

Leaving The Way He Came In

He died
curled in a fetal position
eyes frozen in wonderment
a question mark
achieving its long sought closure.

I saw the signs
along the way
his body turning in on itself
his hands clenched at his side
cramped into blunt fists
the square shoulders
arcing downward
forming a hump of heavy burden.

The years
left him
a wizened infant
with wisps of fine gray hair
springing from his scalp
as if
to finally transcend him.

I sat beside his hospital bed
a prison of metal rails
a terminal crib
where he was nursed in shifts
breast fed with IV tubes
lulled to sleep
by the beep of the incessant monitor.

He passed
mouth gaping
wearing the indignity of a diaper
navel gazing
into eternity.

3 A.M. On The Psychiatric Ward

My flashlight beamed
on the usual bed bound bodies
breathing under layers.
Then -
in the middle of the hall
she came running towards me
perfect, unblemished...naked
a nocturnal melodrama unfolding
the embodiment of a wet dream.
Her eyes beamed
sensitive as a Doe's -

then she lunged for me -
I grabbed both of her arms
and we did our strange dance
anointed by moonlight
from the barred window
tripping the light fantastic -
I was frightened and thrilled,
as she took the lead.

The Death Of Bernie M.

I remember
it was his typical saunter
down the locked ward
the vague
cusp of a smile
a black,
shopworn suit
looking like a down-at-the-heels
clergyman,
the benign muttering
for yet another
cigarette.

And so suddenly
his mouth gaping
at the ceiling
his eyes
already void of life
the machine
throwing shocks
through his vacant
body -
How delighted he
would be

to see a pretty nurse
covering his mouth
with her full lips
the surprise with me -
straddling him
pressing desperately
on his chest...
What a shame
all this...
waited
for his
corpse.

On The Ward: Stuffed Animals

At night
as you
check the rooms
the flashlight discovers
these animals
attached to grown
women -
like suckling babes
held tightly
against the darkness -
memories of morning
abandonment -
the deep chasms
that were never
bridged.
On these lonely
nights
any union
will do.

Zero

And what is
its purpose?
Simply
to mock
the finite?
A dead-end
where we can't
avoid -
the void.

The horrible truth
of those
muttered
antiquated prayers
"Ashes to Ashes,
Dust to Dust,"
And
whether we
want to
face it
or not
we must...
we must.

My First Poetry Reading

It was when
I broke into
my father's
liquor cabinet
his celebratory
Chivas Regal
coursing through

my veins.
My tirade
on the manicured lawn
A hot Summer
Long Island evening
my neighbors
a transfixed audience
lining Revere Street
as I performed
screamed
my screed
against the suburbs
the conspiracy of broad lawns
and narrow minds
my invective breaking through
the drone of crickets
the deadening murmur
of TV sets
through open windows -
my madcap struggle
with the taciturn and very focused
police
on the lawn -

Hung over
and relishing
my performance
at dawn.

Portrait Of My Mother During Her Solitary Meal

She never thought
she would miss the fights.
But now,

she hears the grinding
of her jaw
the crack of bones
the marrow coats
her coated tongue.
The radio's chattering drone
the lonely voices from the hinterlands
that she giddily mocked with him -
are her's
now.

And the photos of him
held tenuously by a cheap magnet
on the refrigerator door
an inanimate taunt
a ridiculously happy frozen
moment of time -
She is now
a prisoner of
deadened silence
What was her crime?

Losing A Stream Of Consciousness On The Dudley Bus

Such a fey day
boarding the bus
staring out the window
at the shell
of the Wursthaus
how they ripped
that dark womb of Watney's and Wurst -
the solitary meals
hidden in the wooden booth
the comfortable barking
of the ancient waitresses.

The bus snakes down Mass. Ave
past the August domes of MIT -
The patrician towers of Beacon Hill
erupt in the distance
like taciturn old Brahmins
amidst the sleek towers
of steel and glass.

The bus turns down Harrison Ave
I remember the Shanty Lounge
the project rats
surprising me from behind
their cunning eyes
so feral
all of
us frozen
in recognition.

It's high noon now
but I squint for more light
to see the elevated tracks once again
the grid work of light and dark
the girders
shaking from
the roar of the metropolis.
I daydream
of the subway cars
and the sun's descent
into the backdrop
of city rooftops -
That din
that I embraced
as a young man...

And finally
I sleep...
Last stop.

Mark Sonnenfeld

(1956 -   )

Uses a variety of compositional methods to create non-linear sequences that impart new visual & conceptual experiences & perspectives. He often uses cut-up & random techniques, mathematically derived word choices, or collage to create his pieces.

flower green repellent tip *a)* spec dualism
: = o no hope. That . . . 3 r u 2 b Academy.
Anchor Invitation Things Mite Supposing Flip Unpublished
Nut-fruit Swell Folk road of the Film Co Quiet America
Country measuring now the air control sizzle
electricals see the way we face Death Tranquility
slow to change urine
Dooplicate Next Be 10 - 12 years dinky
Classical record set . . . ganza ballet
PRETENDING TO BE SOMETHING
ELSE OLD DARKENS MACHINE
What is shyD CRAZU have a black cause wax
deceased at funerals *likings* st on the part
flips a switch
in the deep everybody's cue no nose diamonds.
He'd go on
Heigh-ho glue anything
all in-between anyway to what I suppose is going
claw style sil crafts this knuckle language at
least in vertigo, alouds, contingency,
scream system*a* hoods pru for the drop
like notes in its analysis from unknown
like there suppose   (ache, pound)

MOCKER TYPES AROUND. Tranquilizer Park
in fact it's made all kinds of clever disservice

Poiz
by   which
me   clearly
uh, Ioddity "ADENT!"
(with a tie) tie pisspoor t
is actually wasp speak?act
is actually evolution
freshairLie   mushroom
d : t ty ? (to control
unkind middle   o

          Scattershitguest o
          , dry
          Nography   Block self
¿   fIR from   worm
          lost
          M   own   brusq.
          SICK   of   landfall

¿   Pauly   Wooduummm
          forgeries   winter   mad
¿   The   simpliest   no-think
          sun does what the sun wants
          I_ Yeah & could maybe piebald

poetry, art

                              the front face of 1035 2nd Avenue
is next to a laundromat
entered by hitting the 2-s button, emily
holds a framed picture -
                              (is curiosity
being afraid of the dark report
while looking up, true sentences come out whenever
the world isnt right/
built from lines in the head
lies 9.3 million in real estate / at that distance
the upper east side
is an otherwise court-appointed beauty mark &)
she strokes her hair
            as if (we don't belong)
            w michael in a box underground
            it is a cold recess, or a warm yellow quilt
            is another sprawled in an armchair
            a streaked face
            for cigarettes downstairs
            of the anaesthesiologist, the overnight at 1035
2nd Avenue, 29 for domestics, 49 for wine
(sidestep to a trafficjam) (2000-foot smoke cloud)
a bakeryline, a 4234th dawn, a psychiatrist
looks out the windows
in a hudson county town
of walls and bridges (and
cheap thing satisfactions no more
than her garden that this is over
hatbands of red counting   10   11   12)

Thump on for head ? , biopsy ?, baloney ?
pP
 Too confusing...
  .50 Minutes ond   foot cavity ,
  Angry *doub* Large Leaf Sway Scarecrow
  mind. (militarygrade)
  blacksunglass   hood,
   brainstem, lumberyard
   teens .
        its , Nor am , a , asocial
       Behavioral teens eve by lumberyard
          'What-up swaz'
    lie-infest governmental thousandfold
    verso
     , -ish & clump sooty <u>um</u> <u>warblers</u>
       I acquiesced shakery , pinup lamp ,
        chewi gum

Sitting

    direction.   a column of doubtful air.
    -BACH 32nd rest   the nostrils of fugue ; body (of

    hiding out)
    out in a trance or something
    I bike unthinkably

             -Braining
        -Is my spectacle
        -Skitter eyeblinks

-Awkwards to talk, I

Who I was   ?
         It's okay
         I blew it
A sidewalk behavior
Deciding to wear
Involuntary

         Whites
                   WAY OFF :   force labor smile   hipp si

                   say-so elephant behavior, birth and death
                            housewifery, children thumb x
                            at understanding !

                   the hand to the side Lostsockets . rig
                   at Life of Study rods -
         (What)
                   A moping moon Author see
                   to No Parking concretes.
                   assembling this   medieval helmet.

Make ovals in the mind-counter clockwise cockatoo prodigal.
Zip by not where is occupied monument dolt debris going
where is (and ways) a candle and WHY-NOT the most direct
so much for that other rag bag distinction fort face. Tubular
cemetery auto immunes snow wham, far cart, fuzz into furthering
end simple name the pit undignified tea-leaves groan stomach
lay two open and empty grade depths not in a raincoat but a free
hand sports the wine list.
     Is not pretty "or - else" vitta or voice must ask whirring please -
forgive. Cylinder thing slaps honest sub standard lighter flame.
Red of the head organs.

Documents?

Wonky shoes can sell freelance. The tape mummy type. Shirt sleeves dumb of bliss 999 without quite three quarters good as dead any adequate for the part blot bush underside china inscription split socket hinges and wrongmatter microphone dark hallS:

> "cautiously not whisper <u>brat</u> / call about matter in
> New York. ibuprofen. Dead Sea bag video ... the
> bell tower cryptic 5% gets to worry courage off the bus
> a gaunt tree on the basis "Turning" at least a line of
> thought cow bell fitted disturbance purr of the meter
> echelons..."

(afterwards)

Vaguely said is a small transmitter subject on the chest to be a little suspicions image heart exclusive specimen zling of the road to go by the words in the cold unimportant police lay and arrange about its earned a string unlike 2step years ago terrific pictures of 3room

1. vomit   dig (pity)
2. reportorial cardboard. old-N$^{\underline{o}}$
3. alien fashion. chords too (ear).
4. mile. people had die.
5. burnt L iron shot. manufacture. 2 cat standoff
6. team. sabotage.
7. surgeon damp dollar.
8. truck claw (judy)
9. Gooney. one of the manhole.
10. is red airfoil is variation.
11. film treatment tablelands.
12. small limp tumble two:nine
13. wait   free.   Ex-ha,
14. I'd accomplish nothing hitching
15. bread before roads.

At of are. Down or g

           suffocating. energy
Pipe.   head "Man"   in   go
Comfortable standing ferry V
sells glass couch Un-cool an
fink shoved pointed "No! ish'
crawl   iron   beat , Why?
Mattresses sour olive heat
command of the Universe I
zero face Contents scramble
Con blink - spine hi Align
period manifest skylight Loc
really$00 It met No think no9
Remember: Egregio owns at
spirit neurotic , initiating tho
expressing frsh momentary c
  all,

            me   Screamed,
Lamp (Then)
had, and in , Sat   that   (,)
the sign (-_)

Naturally some cans.
Stone chronicles.
"Duck looking Up."
Double bass its lower part beautified bide
triangle –, – weren't beats
off with self unlooking attainer grabs ironbars

269

and onionskin (Another thought:
could be 10243 Berlin standing in
the middle hand directed hand in silence
but this is important dopey unspeak nod
bitty twisted press j and i believing)

:::::::::::::::::::::: "
levels" + "any stars inside" ceiling cuts both ways
diminished POEM PEEPS 02[8;26
comatose © toast o crackling the
puffs
pOster xi cottons please optical comet its
image
        image Out o'c   Remorse no nuts
down = not on- ♥ , goes darkness Unit vs.
what ? seat to the batwriter alone thick muz
brain,
thing was a real solid silent wrong concentration
bleed
standard or — sun little flubs of disguise

raindog

How to do a movie division drill.

She spun around the brass pole.

Height: 5'8"

Dress size

I worked in a steel mill four years.

I can burn. Of the American male before beginning

the exercise ran rain on Eighth

Avenue TV.

TV The Killing Rocks Park Trashiness
face the sky yanking go and holding
to a street corner stereotype. I pumped out endless articles.
To guess that's one way to put
the flattened cardboard in some kind cockeye
there's a ton a good European which too I have
otherwise made through any media appeared glassy like
it was almost tradition. Pals. Mouth. Modern art -teas to
 thought
turtleneck of a way to live venetian haircuts was dead and
alive

                              soft sorry cotton einstein
and the ballerina body mystiques, standbys, screw-ups
replaying in the mind X-rays.

Corner:

names skintight to's anonymous station mis-
carried all applause RE: is nothing this world
anymore draining poor diary attribute strife
underneath influences unlikely mysterious support
and love? Too insecure a cosmetic bitbackground
outside double. It doesn't represent anything
special. Birds than their music. Withdraw
floating. Riot date to the all blah.
        11 spot screaming link skirt like a revved
revoltingly dirty delinquent interested of the
really – although in any way - lenox portrait.

Balls rolling. Owl fork. Mind mirrors work in
pair untilreplaying in the mind X-rays
managing at this point has not (an established
center) locked in this spot thereby masking a
seesaw frame toothcap bad and well television
the get-up try languaged that who is intervening
how enter pulling mouthcorners join it's feel
pile up marks knife mime brag fixate eclipse
a frozen horseshoe. Made the practice page damp
straightforward rope route damn modus operandi
for how a man flat pulp felliniesque was
nonetheless draped - pallen suit fully auspicious
elude now corridor odd whereabout not sits a
barge found acting slam throwaway say hello, no-
bodies, mystiques, standbys, screw-up, telling
lies, rejection cockeye syrupy tow tight shoot.

Down next
The subject Vilma

In limited rain. I know it.
A blackie raindog is crafty
But not even close
regardless, at the least, the lost
and at the last all free loves to hate.
Jeez I imagine. I browse wet
at the killing rocks park, not to certify
An alcohol to drink, you know
The verse : By then softer hair
But don't quote me

Of the blind date
LOOKS : of go and holding sounds
wack-like
@ satiric loiterers portray, Here it's 8
of them, I wore the blitzkrieg workjacket
okay
forever a foot function
throwing a pebble I reexamine less.

++ IT.

++ IT.

++

++it is   victim of mistaken identity
erroneous hurl satellite by on second
vapor vowel readability ultraviolt, sl
layouts a mimicked design into disflo
x change photocopies ten seconds to ast
Videot   ˥
Furnace Λ¿ difficult shadow great feel loos
Worktri   me & y. walking around inside
Television Head Room Board Rude Street For TheV
oice Liss Composition Front Microphone
Signal Other Permission Event
z   anecdotal. speak side   _
doxical   ; ' reality ' sale low idea knife estoft
painted itself - / -   -   i
                        .
People "NO" hang

Breathing straw   harbor
                    'jfo½
39edl   0048tpg   .   cj   fpwk½ - 1 i̱oo°
                1±±jq.   0395vn
                    ?.

            a2pk;½
                            : .

        □   jalk
                                    jekurd

        iss   of   ;   botch   old   nephew

            Zimmermen sprechen asphalt gogo
oaf.   By   side   or   close.   Absently   eat   some
sort of explosion

Ains   Toilet stand   ;
ad lib /s/   By: And sneak
wheeldie   s   cone 2 a libertine
bat destinatario   priz undervalue in le   □
srew
        z
citilcorp yrots   knighthood gazehound
the line count carbon + surname the dart
aside.

improvising with broken dohers

(ARCHIVE. o I can play the clue
totallye smog beethoven marko job pin
this creation of DR LONDON looks real-study
a howl hyde toole

↗ entry of the earth.
sea lanes maintain taproot hornet wake
black cat beret
cool bygone
crusty underdog hear t i n
`d BohemianTHERE IS CHARGE!'
Big Extra Wo
motto <u>n</u> or <u>m</u> the tongue flattens my mouth
-and
jewel works ,while animals substituted
on hooks
Lastnight drama blows clearOs halo beam
We The People Sax!
(which I no-faced sax) SO at the moss Shrine
ride it differently
a short one-act NOTEBOOK JETTISON
BURIAL MAN: "A day ended up a
lonely gulp. Ever notice the hopes
of gravity, some of the new-gravity?"
LYINGWOMAN: (Humming,   Metropolitan collar
and mental fool)   "I perform on white
flowers so called trite footsteps."

ohm, pond, moon composition.

                                        -strap
on belly searchlight. r e l a x : its planet basement

stori oneword kook dialogue, low clouds,
flugelhorned
strangulated paces within re telling jag-jag play-tonguing
my floyd voices
all lo-fi

nanoseconds

(here umbrella hid)   Time.
                                    Toilets.
eating up hypersensitivity storms had love, or the like
                                    parking secretly

-experience
Guesswork stack is about
the scary twist, luck / evil

Ye
I will in a nom de plume
I will survive (surely drag) calculating neither hideous
          nor deep a
Sinkable
Nowhere / Everywhere
knee, lung, angst, mock, um, er, yawn some gas
bicycle ly sublime down Oconee Street repeating

Hoo!
Cold
CLOAK

Hi   + / -
An Pion Street of the individual presto
Point   1 / 3rd
Attitude.

276

Rid its the arrival
SHOUTING OUT OUT LOUD POETRY MARK FLAT
ROOF
OF THE syllabus   accordions (there two)

Sleep   uunnhh
i   lov
3   egg
Photograf of drain , Lifestrike , ink <u>h</u>
<u>Abstract</u> : 8   mirr
                little children
EXACTL DAPPLE EYE EVIL MORAL FORMULA CRYING

<u>HEY</u> <u>YOU</u>

thoughts   7.14.00   (for dave)

Dog + fish   (*)   english fraught
educate man imitating
less dumb get smarts, hum headed
H a   h a d to learn everybodys
Terrific!   *What?*
no shit, oddities belong : the life go
You see on the walls in the mens room
You see in the occurring modern Boom-Boom
Age   O I will stand

277

fun (I think so) I do
scratch my stomach
hornswoggle I hear
in the distance compound physical play

on 2 separate meanings •

Another : Im interested in types. (& I write about it
shit)
Simply get-out of your Mind

simply books and magazines and articles
simply dream the problem w/ millions of american
mirrors
said-geometrical reality pushing and shoving
dizzy variations, and some fields of wisdom are also
a drag

No. 1   truth   (or myth)

Human BEings are sensitive rods
Record much of the best photography
And - - - insofar, communication

Vh dden transmitterunderio

rehsiLd-

F a t ramaticalil therm a n (, s}ckjeep (., nHorndo

Av   oid it self blo wfl i   T

Track Douglas   hybrid   room mate ∪ s

⊥e

Slang

       -

    . .

2 teena
Public
With a   camera
and fo   h.
Echo: . . . erasures,   . . era-o.!or ot ale-
Los O   ce Ac   ho
Bing el   ,
Nana: Perf.
Its (Weir   dno)
you can   llburr N
shade   told   sLac. ,
Echo: ivalent   (e:ow) o para-
apple st   p, 99-
Nana: ou wo   no $$
want!   (neeze)
my hero
eyelashes   fAll off
at midn   ht jump-
            (sneeze)   (resplendent) (journalistic)

spray-paint grafitti U know bat-life artistry
ext.
BACKtooth.

.

.   i sHall agi- ' tate ' a ccent

                    giveout HOW TO

DON'T SAY
CHAINS
& by a Monument parting shot :
bootbeats. recordbooks. badtemper.

: symbol t autobiographic part - - -

dO the shifty eye cry
Shelllife
Slouch
Rule
Tub
Dop
Dodder   [beats too man
in trampled grass

- ' nonsense '   ]

:

Richard Morris

(1939 - 2003)

Used humor & absurdity to comment on a world of deteriorating values. He combined colloquial language with surrealistic imagery & reference to public icons to express his uniquely intelligent persona.

Reno, Nevada

In Reno, Nevada the old ladies play slot
          machines and never stop.
Reno, Nevada has an efficient police
          force, an annual rodeo, and an
          active Chamber of Commerce,
Reno, Nevada was named after a Paiute
          Indian chief called Reno, Nevada.
General U.S. Grant wanted to be buried
          in Reno, Nevada.
Guiseppe Verdi wrote an opera called
          "Reno, Nevada."
When Jesus Christ was nailed to the cross,
          he cried out, "Reno, Nevada!"

Sometimes I awake suddenly from strange
          dreams: like some huge beast, Reno,
          Nevada is crawling toward me across
          the desert.

The Death Of Mozart

Then the baboons bolted, and zebras
ran into trees; the sky turned gold
and a red moon lit up mountains.

A somber voice said "Mozart", and
pigeons shat on the world; the voice
added, "died", and aardvarks smiled.

The musicians sat stiffly and dreamed
of orgies; flutists thought of beer,
the oboeists of sodomy, only the horn

players mourned. When Mozart died,
he became the world; notes flooded the air
like swollen streams and a flock of Cupids
dragged Don Juan from hell.

Hope Is The Thing With Feathers
That Perches In The Soul

After his mind was consumed he
went around converting Jehovah's
Witnesses and sniffing
cocker spaniels; he thought of
going into Real Estate, and demanded
of cabooses how they knew they existed.

What happened to him has
happened to us all; like
us, he blew his neurons
out hoping life would come back
with some kind of free
gift, or a surprise ending.

Rimbaud

Rimbaud
once quoted
Tarzan

as saying, "Who
greased
my vine?"

9.

In a region only few
can reach Einstein
and Ginsberg sat
exchanging visions.
Neither understood much
of what the other
said. At last they
looked down on the suffering
world: Ginsberg
smoked dope and
Einstein played
his violin.

12.

I'm walking down streets, going in
doorways, jumping out windows, looking
for words. I sit at a window and look

at the street. I try out my eye, I
bounce it on rooftops. I say life
is a lot of nonsense. I fall

in love anyway. I look at the
clouds, they refuse to fall
down. I wander into movies.

Projection booths explode.

13.

A fog comes at
night, it gouges my

brain, it collects
in my eyesockets. My

head fills with thoughts
that are romantic or

silly, that smell
like hotelsigns. I

look at the street,
my eyes feel like Brahms.

For Sharon

light
brown, your

eyes , the ways
they light

on things,
the way your

mind goes,
love, touching

me
(touching)

The Baseball Game

GOD and some of his ANGELS are attending a New York
Yankees baseball game. It is the bottom of the ninth
inning. There are two outs. The Yankees trail by a score
of 13-0.

GOD: It sure is a shitty game.

Suddenly the Yankees come alive. They win.
The next day all the papers describe the
result as a miracle.

The Tail

A MAN is watching a football game on television.
A WOMAN, obviously his wife, is standing at the window.

WOMAN: Honey, come and look.

MAN: Look at that pass.

WOMAN: There's a tail hanging down out of the sky.

MAN: Huh?

WOMAN: There's a tail hanging down out of the sky.

MAN: You're crazy. Can't you see I'm watching a game.

WOMAN: I think it's wagging.

MAN: (Groans)

WOMAN: Come and look.

Suddenly the TAIL comes crashing through the window, killing the WOMAN. The MAN looks briefly over his shoulder, then goes back to the game.

The Pearly Gates

HUMPHREY BOGART stands before the Pearly Gates. A CHOIR OF ANGELS is singing somewhere. Slowly the Gates open, revealing St. Peter, who is PETER LORRE.

PETER LORRE: I bet you have more respect for me now.

Slowly and majestically, God strides forward. God is SIDNEY GREENSTREET. The CHOIR OF ANGELS is singing His praises. He starts to say something, but He can't be heard; the ANGELS are making too much noise. He motions to them to be quiet, then turns back to BOGART.

SIDNEY GREENSTREET: This isn't what you expected, is it, motherfucker?

Socrates

SOCRATES lies asleep. He is dreaming of
three blind mice. They all run after the
farmer's wife. She cuts off their tails
with a carving knife. When he wakes up,
he won't be able to get someone
into a dialogue about it.

288

The Horse

A huge wooden horse stands outside the gates
of a walled city. Two days pass, during which
nothing happens. By this time the horse has
begun to reek of urine. Mutterings begin to
come from its belly. Such as "Who's crazy
idea was this, anyway?" And "Watch out
where you put that sword, asshole!"

The Rabbits

Act I
A MAN and a WOMAN sit in a living room. The MAN is
drunk.

MAN: Did I ever tell you why I was never in the service?

WOMAN: Fred, I was looking at the rabbits.

MAN: They said I was 4-F. There was nothing wrong with me.
I...

WOMAN: Fred, I know. I was out there watching the rabbits.
They were...doing things to each other.

MAN: There was nothing wrong with me at all. But I have this
navel that's six inches to one side, so they figured....

WOMAN: I know, Fred. I was telling you, the rabbits were
doing things to each other. Don't you think...

MAN: All it was, was a bellybutton six inches off. It wasn't like
there was something really wrong with me.

WOMAN: Fred, the rabbits. If we don't do something, we'll wind up with a whole yard full of rabbits.

MAN: Six inches to one side. That's the only reason.

WOMAN: Fred!

MAN: Huh?

Act II
Same scene. The man IS A LITTLE DRUNKER.

WOMAN: Fred, did you feed the rabbits?

MAN: Sure

WOMAN: They're making a racket. They sound like they're hungry.

MAN: I fed them.

WOMAN: Maybe you didn't feed them enough. It isn't like when we had just two of them.

MAN: I fed them a lot.

WOMAN: Maybe you ought to feed them some more. Or go out and take a look at them, or something.

MAN: Sure. Did I ever tell you about how I was 4-F?

WOMAN: Fred, the rabbits.

MAN: All it was, I have this navel...

Act III

Same setting. The man is yet a little drunker. He is sitting in a chair as the WOMAN comes running into the room, slamming the door behind her.

WOMAN: Fred!

MAN: Huh?

Before either can say anything more, the door falls crashing to the floor, and thousands of hungry RABBITS burst into the room. The RABBITS devour both the MAN and the WOMAN. As they do, there are lots of horrible crunching noises.

The Board Of Directors

A BOARD OF DIRECTORS sits around an ostentatiously large table in a corporate board room.

CHAIRMAN: Gentlemen, incredible as it may seem, we are forced to accept the fact that two of the Corporation's largest buildings have been transformed into pineapples.

1st BOARD MEMBER: How is that possible?

CHAIRMAN: We don't know. It isn't even certain that we have any way of finding out. When dealing with events as fantastic as these, one hardly knows where to begin.

2nd BOARD MEMBER (lights a cigar): Is it the work of radicals?

CHAIRMAN: A number of groups have attempted to take credit for it. Personally, I think that it was as much a surprise to them as it was to us. But gentlemen, let me continue. I want to fill you in on the various kinds of action that we're taking. We filed claims with our insurance companies at home, of course. Our legal staff, however, advises us that, given the uniqueness of these recent events, it is probable that we will have to conduct prolonged litigation before we can entertain any hope of collecting. The insurance companies will, in all probability, claim that these occurrences are Acts of God not covered by the policies they issued.

3rd BOARD MEMBER: Ridiculous.

4th BOARD MEMBER: Two buildings. That's a lot of pineapple. Can we sell the juice?

CHAIRMAN: We're looking into that. But it seems that the Food and Drug Administration is preparing to obtain an injunction. They claim that the juice would be a health hazard, that it might turn back into a building at any moment.

1st BOARD MEMBER: Ridiculous. Pineapple juice doesn't turn into steel and concrete.

CHAIRMAN: I think we could make a case for that. Unfortunately, there's another complication. Both buildings were occupied at the time that the events in question took place. We've tunneled into both, but we have been unable to recover any bodies. Our teams encounter nothing but pineapple.

3rd BOARD MEMBER: The employees turned into pineapple too?

The ceiling has begun to leak in a corner of the room. None of the BOARD MEMBERS notice it.

CHAIRMAN: We have no way of knowing (a drop of liquid falls on the table in front of the CHAIRMAN. He ignores it.) As I said, the events are unique. But if we did attempt to market either the pineapple or the juice, I'm afraid that we should have quite a number of lawsuits on our hands.

More liquid drips from the ceiling and falls on the table. The BOARD OF DIRECTORS looks up.

5th BOARD MEMBER: Something ought to be done about that.

CHAIRMAN: Gentlemen, I suggest that we adjourn to another room.

One of the BOARD MEMBERS dips his finger into the liquid and tastes it. The CHAIRMAN and the rest of the BOARD OF DIRECTORS follow suit. At once there is a lot of yelling and screaming and a mad rush for the door. Before the BOARD OF DIRECTORS can get out of the room, however, a torrent of pineapple juice comes crashing through the ceiling. Quickly, the cries die away and everything is calm.

from **The Adventures Of God**

The king's problem was a monster. And I mean a real monster, not a bear that was stealing food from picnic tables, or a coyote that was making off with lambs. This monster was *big*, and it looked like something out of a horror movie. It wouldn't be too inaccurate to say that it looked like a cross between Godzilla and The Swamp Thing.

Well, I'm sure you know how these things are. One day, everything seems so peaceful that nobody dreams that anything is going to happen. The next day, the monster makes an appearance, and before you know it, people are running in all directions, screaming in terror. I'm sure it will come as no surprise that the events in the story I'm about to relate more or less fits this pattern.

Before the monster appeared, life in the kingdom had been quite idyllic. In fact, it seemed that there had never been a people so happy and so prosperous. For a while, the kingdom had been threatened by enemies. But the king and his warriors had gone out to do battle with them, and had been victorious. The enemies had been slaughtered, and an era of peace had begun. After that, the king gradually enlarged his territory. His kingdom was a little bigger every year. As it grew, powerful fighting men flocked to him. Soon he had become so illustrious a monarch that no one in the surrounding realms dared to offer him any trouble. Neighboring monarchs were always offering their daughters to the king, and sending gifts and tribute of various kinds. Gold. Silver. Cattle. Hilariously misshapen dwarfs. Things like that.

The king had gone to a lot of trouble to establish his supremacy, and now he intended to enjoy life. So he gathered together all the slaves he had acquired in his wars, and borrowed some more slaves from neighboring kings, and set them to work building the best and biggest beer bash hall the world had ever witnessed. Or at least that was how it was described by the king's bard, who had a fondness for alliteration.

When the beer hall was completed, the king gave a great feast for his fighting men. Meat and ale were served in abundance, and the bard sang of the king's exploits while accompanying himself on a stringed instrument. The bard's poetry really wasn't very good, but no one paid much attention. They were too busy drinking themselves into a stupor. Anyway, poetry wasn't anything you were supposed to pay much attention to. It was simply there in the background, like Muzak at the supermarket.

I don't think I have to tell you that the little men in the

warrior's heads were in ecstasy. They had never found themselves swimming in so much alcohol. The only drawback was that they couldn't savor the experience as much as they would have liked. The alcohol was a bit too much for them in the end. One by one, they lapsed into unconsciousness.

The feast should have been the high point of the king's career. But it didn't turn out that way. It seems that the monster had been lurking nearby, and that it had taken note of the celebration. For a while, it bided its time. Then, in the dead of night, it struck. It went lumbering toward the beer hall and crashed through the heavy oaken doors. By the time the king's men were able to rouse themselves from their drunken stupor, it had already killed thirty of them. When the warriors opened their eyes, they saw the monster sitting on its haunches in the middle of the hall, eating. The sight was terrifying. Every time the creature took a bite from a man it had killed, there was a horrible crunching noise. It didn't even bother to gnaw the meat off the bones. It would simply rip off an arm or a leg and stuff the bloody limb into its mouth whole, or bite off a head, or crunch on the torso...

I don't suppose I really have to tell you what happened the next day. There was weeping and lamentation throughout the kingdom. The little man in the king's head was especially sad to see that so many fine men had been devoured. He allowed his body to weep copiously as it ordered that the estates of the dead warriors be confiscated and that their stores of ale be brought to the hall...

Now it so happened that the king of this overseas realm had a nephew who was a very large and powerful warrior. He was so big, in fact, that he could have played tackle for the Chicago Bears. He was strong too, and had proved to be practically invincible in battle...

...like her son, the mother was an aquatic monster. She lived at the bottom of a nearby lake. The little man decided that the best course of action was the most straightforward one. He would have Jerry dive into the lake

295

after her...

  ...Jerry jumped into the lake and sank from sight. Five minutes passed. And then ten minutes. And then twenty. By the time a half hour had gone by and Jerry had not resurfaced, everyone was convinced that he was dead...

  But then, about an hour after Jerry had jumped into the lake, the water began to churn, and a red froth rose to the surface...and then (Jerry) began wading toward shore and they saw that he was holding something aloft in one hand. It was the monster's head.

  Time passed (and) eventually Jerry died. When he did, the heirs staged the most splendid funeral the world had ever known. And then they began murdering one another, trying to gain control of Jerry's kingdom.

  None of the survivors was ever able to gain supremacy over the others, however, and the kingdom finally broke up. Nor did the kingdoms that were carved out of it last very long either. These were soon overrun by the Celts. Since the Celts cared little about the monarchs who had ruled in this land before them, Jerry's exploits were quickly forgotten. They were preserved only in some poetry that a few motheaten bards continued to chant. Jerry's deeds, in other words, had become mythical. Before long, no educated person believed that they had really happened.

Contributor's Notes

Stanley Nelson is the author of 11 published books of poetry. He is best known for his long narrative poems, *Idlewild, The Brooklyn Book of the Dead, The Travels of Ben Sira, Nightriffer* & the 4-volume *Immigrant.* He is a graduate of the University of Vermont. He lives in Brooklyn, New York.

Hugh Fox, Ph.D., is the author of over 80 books, most recently *Time & Other Poems* (Presa Press, 2005) & *Blood Cocoon - Selected Poems of Connie Fox* (Presa Press, 2005). He is a Professor Emeritus of American Thought & Language at Michigan State University. He holds a Ph.D. from the University of Illinois. He was a co-founder of COSMEP & is a frequent contributor to the *Small Press Review.* He was the editor of the avant-garde litmag *Ghost Dance* for 4 decades. He is the author of an acclaimed book on pre-Columbian religion & lives in East Lansing, Michigan.

Kirby Congdon is the author of numerous collections of poetry, prose poetry, letters & plays. He is a graduate of Columbia University. He has been the poetry editor for *Cayo* & is a regular contributor to the *Small Press Review.* He recently received a grant from the Anne McKee Artists' Fund to finish a collection of his short plays which will be published by Presa Press in 2006 under the title *God Is Dead (again).* He divides his time between Key West, Florida & Fire Island, New York.

Richard Kostelanetz is the foremost artist of spatial poetry in the last 50 years. His visual & experimental poetry has paved the way for successive writers's exploration of form & content. He is a graduate of Columbia University & a Fulbright Scholar. His work has appeared in numerous artistic venues & has earned him awards and recognition for his diffuse approach to literature. He has produced works including holograms, audiotapes, videotapes, & static visual art. He has been the editor of the litmag *Assembling* & has had numerous independent press publications over the last 4 decades. He continues to live in New York, New York.

Lyn Lifshin has written more than 100 books and edited 4 anthologies of women writers. Her poems have appeared in most of the litmags in the USA. A graduate of Syracuse University & the University of Vermont, she has taught poetry & prose writing for many years at universities, colleges & high schools. She is the recipient of numerous awards including the Jack Kerouac Award for her book *Kiss The Skin Off*. She is the subject of an award-winning documentary film, *Lyn Lifshin: Not Made of Glass*. A new collection of her poetry, *In Mirrors*, will be published by Presa Press in 2006. She lives in Vienna, Virginia.

Harry Smith who wishes to avoid confusion with other Smiths, uses the literary persona of SMITH. A graduate of Brown University, a poet & essayist, he has been the publisher of *The Smith* & the author of 14 books, most recently *The Sexy Sixties* (Birch Brook Press, 2002). He has received the Small Press Center's lifetime achievement award & PEN's Medwick Award. He is nearing completion of his *Light Memoirs: Making the Best of Death*. Recent magazine publications include *Confrontation, The Iconoclast, Prairie Schooner & Presa*. Smith divides his time almost equally between Downeast Maine & Brooklyn, New York.

Eric Greinke is the author of 20 books of poetry, social commentary, fiction & creative non-fiction, most recently *The Drunken Boat & Other Poems From The French of Arthur Rimbaud* (Presa Press, 2005). He has been active in the independent press as the editor of *Amaranthus, Metamorphosis & The Brown Penny Review*, was the founder of Pilot Press Books in the '70s, & an early member of COSMEP. He has worked in the Poets-in-the-Schools program & as a critic for the *Grand Rapids Sunday Press*. He is the founder of Presa Press in 2002. He has a Master's degree in Social Work from Grand Valley State University & lives at Bostwick Lake, Michigan.

John Keene is the author of numerous works of poetry, fiction & prose. He is a Harvard graduate & has a MFA degree from New York University. He has received 4 Pushcart Prize nominations, AGNI Literary Journal's 2000 John Cheever Short Fiction Prize & the 2001 Solo Press/SOLO Magazine Poetry Prize. His writings have appeared in many publications, including most recently *Bridge,* *Fence* & *Nocturnes*. He is currently working on several long fictional works. He lives in Jersey City, New Jersey & teaches at Brown University in Rhode Island.

Lynne Savitt studied poetry with Diane Wakoski in the early 70's & taught writing workshops at various colleges, community centers & prisons. She is the recipient of the Madeline Sadin Poetry Award from *The New York Quarterly*. Her first poem was published in *Playgirl* magazine in 1974. Since that time, her work has appeared in numerous litmags, including *13th Moon, Home Planet News* & *Presa*. She has co-edited *Gravida* & currently co-edits *Caprice*. Her most recent book is

The Deployment of Love in Pineapple Twilight (Presa Press, 2005). She lives on Long Island, New York.

A. D. Winans was the editor & publisher of *Second Coming Magazine/Press* for 17 years. He is a graduate of San Francisco State University, & the author of over 40 books of poems, including *The Holy Grail: The Charles Bukowski Second Coming Revolution* (Dust Books). His work has appeared internationally & been translated into 8 languages. His most recent book is *This Land Is Not My Land* (Presa Press, 2005). He continues to live in San Francisco, California.

Doug Holder is the founder of the Ibbetson Street Press & the former president of Stone Soup Poets. His poetry & articles have appeared in the *Small Press Review, Harvard Mosaic, Heeltap, Sub-Terrain, Main Street Rag, The Boston Globe*, & many others. He holds an M.A. from Harvard University. His interviews with contemporary poets are archived at the Lamont Library at Harvard University. He currently works as a mental health counselor at McLean Hospital, & has run poetry groups for psychiatric patients there for over a decade. He continues to reside in Somerville, Massachusetts.

Mark Sonnenfeld is an experimental writer/mail artist/audio collagist/small press publisher. He has been active on the international scene for over a decade, producing many solo projects as well as collaborating extensively with writers, artists & photographers. He is the founder of Marymark Press. He lives in East Windsor, New Jersey.

Richard Morris, Ph.D., was the author of more than 20 books, including 15 that explain the intricacies of science to the general public. Among these are *Artificial Worlds, Achilles in the Quantum Universe, Cosmic*

*Questions, The Edges of Science, The Nature of Reality,
& Time's Arrows.* He was the editor of *Camels Coming*
magazine & published books under the Camels Coming
Press imprint. His books have been translated into 11
foreign languages. He held a Ph.D. in physics from the
University of Nevada, & was a member of the Society for
the History of Alchemy & Chemistry. He was an original
member & the Coordinator of COSMEP. He lived in San
Francisco, California until his death in 2003 just before
the release of *The Last Sorcerers.* He worked tirelessly
in behalf of independent publishing for 40 years.

Roseanne Ritzema is the assistant editor of
Presa Press & the litmag *Presa.* *Inside The Outside* is
her first book. She is a graduate of Michigan State
University with a Master's degree in Social Work.

Also Available From Presa Press

Selected Poems 1972 - 2005
Eric Greinke
ISBN: 0-9740868-7-8, perfectbound paperback, 140 pgs.,
$12.00
ISBN: 0-9740868-8-6, hardcover, 140 pgs., $18.00
*The best of 33 years. Painterly & surreal, personal poetry
that stretches language both in & out.*

Blood Cocoon - Selected Poems
Connie Fox (a.k.a. Hugh Fox)
ISBN: 0-9740868-9-4, perfectbound paperback, 72 pgs.,
$10.00
*Fox transcends gender & time lines to get in touch with
the Great Mother Goddess. An innovative & powerful
instant classic.*

Time & Other Poems
Hugh Fox
Saddle-stitched paperback, 44 pgs., $6.00
*These poems occupy a space somewhere between auto-
biographical journalism & Jungian dreamwork.*

Selected Poems & Prose Poems
Kirby Congdon
ISBN: 0-9772524-0-X, perfectbound paperback, 84 pgs.,
$10.00
*Congdon's poems address universal themes in colloquial
yet lyric language. The best of 50 years, selected by the
author at the age of 80.*

This Land Is Not My Land
A. D. Winans
Saddle-stitched paperback, 48 pgs., $6.00
Poems of elegant simplicity & honesty by one of our best poets.

The Deployment of Love in Pineapple Twilight
Lynne Savitt
Saddle-stitched paperback, 48 pgs., $6.00
Thirty-six perceptive new poems of feminine strength & sensuality. Her most mature work to date.

Upcoming in 2006
God Is Dead (again)
Plays by Kirby Congdon
ISBN: 0-9772524-2-6, Perfectbound paperback, $15.00.

In Mirrors
Poems by Lyn Lifshin
ISBN: 0-9772524-3-4, Perfectbound paperback, 84 pgs., $12.00

Free S & H on all direct orders from the publisher.
PRESA :S: PRESS
PO Box 792
Rockford MI 49341
presapress@aol.com
www.presapress.com

Printed in the
United States of America
on acid-free
recycled paper.